DISCARD

PEOPLES AND CULTURES OF AFRICA

EAST AFRICA

Edited by Peter Mitchell

CHELSEA HOUSE
PUBLISHERS
An imprint of Infobase Publishing

Chelsea House
An imprint of Infobase Publishing
132 West 31st Street
New York, NY 10001

Library of Congress Cataloging-in-Publication Data

Peoples and cultures of Africa / edited by Peter Mitchell.
    p. cm.
    "Authors, Amy-Jane Beer ... [et al.]"—T.p. verso.
    Includes bibliographical references and index.

    Set ISBN 0-8160-6260-9 (acid-free paper)

Nations & Personalities of Africa ISBN 0-8160-6266-8
Peoples and Cultures of Southern Africa ISBN 0-8160-6265-X
Peoples and Cultures of Central Africa ISBN 0-8160-6264-1
Peoples and Cultures of East Africa ISBN 0-8160-6263-3
Peoples and Cultures of West Africa ISBN 0-8160-6262-5
Peoples and Cultures of North Africa ISBN 0-8160-6261-7

    1. Africa—Civilization. 2. Ethnology—Africa. I. Beer, Amy-Jane. II. Mitchell, Peter, 1962-
        DT14.P46 2006
        960—dc22

                                        2006040011

Chelsea House books are available at special discounts when purchased in bulk quantities for businesses, associations, institutions, or sales promotions. Please call our Special Sales Department in New York at (212) 967-8800 or (800) 322-8755.

You can find Chelsea House on the World Wide Web at
http://www.chelseahouse.com

Printed and bound in China

10 9 8 7 6 5 4 3 2 1

CPHS
LSB
$32.00

For The Brown Reference Group plc.
Project Editor: Graham Bateman
Editors: Peter Lewis, Virginia Carter
Cartographers: Darren Awuah, Mark Walker
Designers: Steve McCurdy, Martin Anderson
Managing Editor: Bridget Giles
Production Director: Alastair Gourlay
Editorial Director: Lindsey Lowe

Consultant Editor
Dr. Peter Mitchell is University Lecturer in African Prehistory, and holds a Tutorial Fellowship in Archaeology at St. Hugh's College, University of Oxford, United Kingdom. He is also Curator of African Archaeology at the Pitt Rivers Museum, Oxford, and an academic member of the multidisciplinary African Studies Centre based at St. Antony's College, Oxford. He has previously worked at the University of Cape Town. He serves on the Governing Council of the British Institute in Eastern Africa and is a member of the editorial boards of numerous journals. From 2004–2006 he held the post of President of the Society of Africanist Archaeologists.

Advisory Editor
Dr. David Johnson is University Lecturer in Comparative and International Education (Developing Countries) and a Fellow of St. Antony's College, University of Oxford, United Kingdom. He is a member of the African Studies Centre, based at St. Antony's College, and has conducted research into education in a wide range of African countries. He serves on the United Kingdom National Commission for UNESCO's working committee on Africa and on the editorial boards of two international journals.

Authors
Matthew Davies
with
Amy-Jane Beer
Richard Vokes

Title page *Samburu dancers (Kenya) with beadwork necklaces.*

CONTENTS

Peoples and Cultures of Africa provides a region-based study of Africa's main ethnic groups, cultures, languages, religions, music, and much more. Five of the six volumes cover large geographical regions, namely: *North Africa, West Africa, East Africa, Central Africa,* and *Southern Africa.* Each of these volumes starts with a series of overview articles covering the political situation today, physical geography, biomes, peoples, cultures, and finally a historical time line. The main articles that follow are arranged A–Z with four types of articles, each distinguished by a characteristic running-head logo and color panel:

ETHNIC GROUPS, such as Maasai, Zulu, Yoruba. Each ethnic group article includes a Fact File and a map, giving the approximate area in which a people mainly live.

MATERIAL CULTURE, such as Contemporary Art, Metalwork, Sculpture, Textiles

PERFORMING ARTS AND LITERATURE, such as African-language Literature, Masks and Masquerade, Dance and Song

RELIGION, SOCIETY, AND CULTURE, such as Islam, Christianity, Marriage and the Family

The sixth volume (*Nations and Personalities*) is divided into three main sections: *Political and Physical Africa* presents a complete overview of Africa, followed by profiles of every nation on the continent; *International Organizations* and *Environmental Organizations* review major international bodies operating in the region; and *African Personalities* gives biographies of some 300 people from throughout Africa.

Within each volume there is a *Glossary* of key terms, lists of *Further Resources* such as other reference books, and useful Web sites. Volume *Indexes* are provided in volumes 1–5, with a complete *Set Index* in volume 6.

EAST AFRICA HAS A FASCINATING HISTORY. LIKELY THE CRADLE OF HUMANKIND, OVER TIME IT HAS SEEN MANY MIGRATIONS OF PEOPLE WITHIN THE REGION AND INFLUXES OF PEOPLE FROM OUTSIDE. WHAT HAS EMERGED IS ONE OF AFRICA'S MOST DIVERSE REGIONS, WITH MORE THAN 250 ETHNIC GROUPS AND ALMOST AS MANY LANGUAGES.

A political map of East Africa. Even one of the poorer countries of the region, Tanzania, has recently secured more investment, with a huge new gold mine opening near Mwanza in 2001. Tanzania is now Africa's third largest producer of gold.

CONFRONTING PROBLEMS

Modern East Africa suffers from a number of problems, some natural and some human made. Many regions, expecially in the dry northeast, remain prone to drought. Drought, along with poverty, has caused famine at times. In April 2005, for example, the World Food Program stepped in to help 850,000 Eritreans at risk of starvation.

Interethnic tensions continue, and governments have proved highly resistant to democratic reform, with corruption rife in many countries. The government of Mwai Kibaki, which took power in Kenya in 2002, promised to tackle corruption but failed to deliver and lost the confidence of the electorate in November 2005, when its reformed constitution was rejected.

Around half East Africa's population lives below the World Bank poverty line, while preventable diseases such as diphtheria, typhoid, typhus, and malaria are major killers. AIDS is a huge problem with around 5 percent of the population HIV positive.

THE REGIONAL ECONOMY

Although urbanization is rapidly continuing, East Africa remains predominantly rural. The vast majority of the population is engaged in subsistence agriculture—growing food simply for their own consumption. There is little industrialization and the major regional exports are coffee and tea; minor exports include sugar, livestock, grain, and horticultural produce. Conflict and corruption have meant that East Africa's mineral resources have been underexploited. Government mismanagement has often resulted in the small profits obtained from mining enterprises going overseas.

Meeting energy requirements has also long been a headache for the region, though new developments, particularly in hydroelectricity, are intended to secure more reliable power generation. These programs include hydroelectric dams in Uganda at

Owen Falls and Bujagali Falls on the Nile, Kenya's Turkwel hydroelectric scheme, and Ethiopian plans to harness the waters of the Blue Nile.

Unemployment is a major problem throughout the region, with educated school leavers outnumbering available jobs by a ratio of 10:1. While educational standards are gradually improving (free primary education exists across much of the region), it remains to be seen how the aspirations of these school leavers will be incorporated into predominantly agricultural economies. Tourism, now one of the region's major sources of foreign income, may represent one solution, though it raises ethical questions: To what extent does wildlife tourism protect or damage already fragile ecologies, and how should supposed "traditional" African cultures not be forced into a static "reality" by the tourist market?

THE ROAD TO RECOVERY

Despite its problems there is a growing optimism that East Africa is on the road to recovery. Civil wars in Burundi and Somalia seem close to resolution, and Rwanda has recovered magnificently from the 1994 genocide through active reconciliation measures. Most countries seem firmly set on the path toward stable multiparty democracy. Importantly it appears likely

that most East African countries will soon meet the criteria by which their crippling international debts will be dropped. The re-establishment of the East African Union between Kenya, Uganda, and Tanzania in 2001 represents an important step forward. East African leaders are increasingly recognizing the need to take the initiative in ensuring the social and economic recovery of the region. Both Kenya and Tanzania have been highly active in solving the problems of neighboring nations, acting as arbitrators and hosting peace talks. There is even some hope that the fragile peace settlement brokered in Kenya for the war-torn country of Somalia, whose government and economy collapsed in 1991, will hold.

Tourists on safari in the Masai Mara reserve in Kenya. East Africa's abundance of wildlife has long proved a draw to Western visitors. In the past, people came to hunt big game, whereas now the aim is to conserve the region's natural history as a precious resource.

Tea picking on a Malawian plantation. East Africa is known for its strong, dark tea, a cash crop introduced in colonial times.

PHYSICAL EAST AFRICA

GEOGRAPHICALLY, EAST AFRICA IS VERY DIVERSE. LOWLAND COASTS STRETCH FROM ERITREA AND DJIBOUTI IN THE NORTH TO TANZANIA IN THE SOUTH. INLAND ARE VAST HIGHLAND MASSIFS, SAVANNA PLAINS, SEMIARID DESERTS, VAST LAKES, AND, IN THE FAR WEST, THE EDGE OF THE TROPICAL RAINFORESTS OF THE CONGO BASIN.

East Africa comprises 10 countries: Malawi, Tanzania (including Zanzibar), Kenya, Uganda, Burundi, Rwanda, Ethiopia, Somalia, Djibouti, and Eritrea.

THE GREAT RIFT VALLEY

Winding its way through East Africa, from the Red Sea in the north, to Mozambique in the south, is the Great Rift Valley. It was created some 20 million years ago by the collision of the Indian Ocean and African tectonic plates (parts of the Earth's crust). This colossal geological feature supports many different environments, including steep escarpments, volcanic moonscapes, and scorching lowland bush. The Rift has helped shape the ethnic and economic mosaic that is East Africa, with hot lowland parts of the Rift suitable only for livestock herding, while the surrounding highlands support crop growing.

THE ETHIOPIAN HIGHLANDS

East Africa comprises a series of highlands interspersed with lower plateaus and plains. These often have their own unique patterns of rainfall and temperature. In Ethiopia, an area measuring some 33,000 square miles (85,000 sq km), is mountainous highland more than 6,500 feet (2,000 m) in altitude. To the northeast is Lake Tana, the source of the Blue Nile, while the Rift Valley runs through the southeast, cutting the highlands in two. To the north the highlands stretch into Eritrea, giving way to the coastal lowlands that border the Red Sea. Because East Africa lacks major navigable rivers, the Red Sea (along with the Indian Ocean) has long been its most important waterway, linking the region to the Mediterranean and the Near East.

PEAKS AND LAKES

To the west the Ethiopian Highlands descend into Sudan, eventually meeting the Nile on its long journey northward. To the east and

Map of the main physical features of East Africa. Extensive savannas make this region abundant in wildlife, especially large mammals. The Great Rift Valley in the west is where humankind originated.

ERITREA
Asmara.
SUDAN
Aksum.
.Mekele
Red Sea
Gondar.
DJIBOUTI
.Djibouti
Gulf of Aden
Lake Tana   ETHIOPIA
Horn of Africa
Blue Nile   Ethiopian   Dire Dawa.
Berbera
.Addis Ababa
Highlands
.Hargeysa
.Asela
SOMALIA
.Goba
White Nile
Shebelle River
Juba River
Lake Turkana
UGANDA   KENYA
.Mogadishu
△ Stanley
Kampala.   .Eldoret
.Kisumu   Tana River
INDIAN OCEAN
Lake Victoria   Kenya △
.Nairobi
.Kigali   Kismaayo
RWANDA
.Mwanza
BURUNDI   Olduvai   △ Kilimanjaro
Gorge
.Bujumbura
Mombasa
Rift Valley   Tanga.
Lake Tanganyika   .Dodoma   Zanzibar Island
TANZANIA
.Dar es Salaam
.Mbeya
Rift Valley
Lake Malawi
MALAWI
Lilongwe.   MOZAMBIQUE
Mozambique Channel

spread southward into the highland ranges of northern Tanzania which include Africa's highest mountain, Mt. Kilimanjaro (19,340 ft; 5,895 m). Both this and Mt. Kenya remain snowcapped throughout the year. Moving south into Tanzania, the Rift Valley becomes a large plateau that stretches east to the coast, westward to Lake Tanganyika, and southward to Lake Malawi. In northwestern Tanzania, and to the west of the Rift, the vast Serengeti savanna plains stretch north into Kenya's Masai Mara. These areas have game reserves that are home to large populations of wildlife, for which East Africa is renowned worldwide. To the southeast, the Rift creates the spectacular volcanic landscape of the crater highlands, including the Ngorongoro crater wildlife reserve and Olduvai Gorge. It was in the Olduvai Gorge that scientists found well-preserved fossils of early hominids (human ancestors), allowing them to trace the origins of humankind to East Africa.

The central highlands of Kenya descend sharply to the west into the Rift. Here, where the valley reaches its narrowest point spectacular escarpments, often up to 4,900 feet (1,500 m) high, are formed. Crossing the dry valley floor the land rises again, forming another series of equally impressive escarpments that ascend to Kenya's Western Highlands. To the southwest these gently descend toward Lake Victoria and the flat plains of Uganda and western Rwanda and Burundi. Running northward out of Lake Victoria, the White Nile passes a series of rapids before flowing into Lake Albert and then through Uganda and on into Sudan. To the west rise the snowcapped peaks of the Ruwenzori Mountains (Mt. Stanley 16,765 ft; 5,110 m), which famously have one of the most significant populations of mountain gorillas. Stretching south into Rwanda and west into the Democratic Republic of the Congo, they mark the boundary between East and Central Africa.

southeast the highlands descend into vast, semiarid plains that stretch to the Gulf of Aden, across Somalia and southward into northeastern Kenya. To the south these highlands merge into plains that extend into northern Kenya, northwestern Uganda, and the Lake Turkana basin. There they butt up against the well-watered and fertile central highlands of Kenya. These highlands center on Mt. Kenya (17,060 ft; 5,199 m), and

The harsh terrain of the Ethiopian highlands allowed its peoples to live in relative isolation from their neighbors. As a result, Christianity there was able to withstand the spread of Islam from the seventh century onward.

EAST AFRICA HAS A VARIETY OF ECOSYSTEMS, INCLUDING MOUNTAINS, PLAINS, DESERTS, AND TROPICAL FORESTS. A CHAIN OF MAJOR LAKES LIES IN THE GREAT RIFT VALLEY THAT RUNS NORTHEAST–SOUTHWEST ACROSS THE REGION. YET A GROWING HUMAN POPULATION IS PLACING HUGE STRAIN ON ENVIRONMENTAL RESOURCES.

TROPICAL GRASSLAND/SAVANNA: SERENGETI

The Serengeti and connected grasslands occupy much of northern and central Tanzania and southern Kenya, extending north into Ethiopia and Somalia. There are two annual wet seasons (March–May and November–December) and a long dry spell from August to October. Bush fires regularly occur there, although the landscape quickly recovers. The main vegetation is tough grass, with hardy, spiny trees such as the acacia. The grasslands are home to much wildlife, including the safari "big five" species (rhino, elephant, leopard, lion, and buffalo), along with huge herds of zebra, wildebeest, and other antelope. Characteristic birds include cattle egrets, oxpeckers, and several species of weaver birds.

DESERT/XERIC SCRUB: HORN OF AFRICA DESERT

The coastal landscape of the Horn of Africa is mostly flat volcanic plain covered with sand or gravel, but it rises sharply in the limestone Somali Highlands. Rain is infrequent and unpredictable. Annual temperatures average between 80 and 91°F (27–33°C) on the coast, but are cooler at altitude. Dorcas gazelle, Salt's dikdik, and Soemmering's gazelle eke out a living on the sparse vegetation of the coastal desert, but there are very few other animals or people. The narrow entrance to the Red Sea is a bird migration route from Asia to Africa and back. Birds of prey are commonplace, with up to 26 species passing through in the fall.

Map labels

SUDAN
ERITREA
Asmara.
Aksum.
.Mekele
Red Sea
Gulf of Aden
DJIBOUTI
.Djibouti
Gondar.
Lake Tana
ETHIOPIA
Horn of Africa
Blue Nile
Ethiopian
Dire Dawa.
.Berbera
.Addis Ababa
Highlands
.Hargeysa
SOMALIA
.Asela
.Goba
Shebelle River
White Nile
Lake Turkana
Juba River
.Mogadishu
UGANDA
KENYA
Kampala.
.Eldoret
.Kisumu
Tana River
INDIAN OCEAN
Lake Victoria
.Nairobi
.Kigali
.Kismaayo
RWANDA
.Mwanza
BURUNDI
Olduvai Gorge
.Bujumbura
Rift Valley
.Mombasa
Tanga.
.Dodoma
Zanzibar Island
Lake Tanganyika
TANZANIA
.Dar es Salaam
.Mbeya
Lake Malawi
MALAWI
MOZAMBIQUE
Lilongwe.
Mozambique Channel
Rift Valley

Legend

- Montane grassland
- Deserts and xeric shrublands
- Tropical and subtropical grasslands, savannas, and shrubland
- Tropical and subtropical moist broadleaf forests
- Flooded grasslands
- Water

Pelicans and flamingos gather on a lake in East Africa's Great Rift valley to feed on plankton from its mineral-rich waters. Many Rift valley lakes contain unique fishes, such as hundreds of species of cichlids.

after the last Ice Age, when the climate at lower altitudes became much hotter. As a result, the highlands are home to a large number of species that are unique to the area, including the world's rarest dog, the Ethiopian wolf, and the giant mole rat. The 9,900 feet (3,000 m) high plateaus are covered in grassy moorland, which boasts a rich diversity of herbs and shrubs.

Farther inland, the upland areas are more hospitable, with open acacia scrub, and dragon and pistachio trees in the shelter of steep valleys and ravines. Similar dry, open woodlands are found farther south in the Maasai scrublands of northern Kenya.

TROPICAL MOIST BROADLEAF FOREST: COASTAL FOREST

The east coast of Africa supports a complex mosaic of habitats—mostly humid forest, swamp (including mangroves), and rich grassland. Plant and animal life is very diverse there, but the whole region is under pressure from human activities, mainly agriculture and tourism. Some 20 species of birds and mammals, including Clarkes' weaver bird, the agile mangabey, and the golden-rumped elephant shrew, are endemic to the forests—meaning they are found nowhere else in the world.

MONTANE GRASSLAND: ETHIOPIAN HIGHLANDS

These ancient volcanic mountains provide a refuge for numerous plant and animal species that died out elsewhere in Africa

FLOODED GRASSLAND

Small patches of rich, seasonally flooded grassland are scattered throughout the East African region. The flood waters prevent the growth of trees and enrich the soils, so when the water recedes, the areas become magnets for grazing animals. Also included within this biome are the salt lakes of Kenya and Tanzania. Their biological value is limited, but they are home to enormous breeding colonies of greater and lesser flamingo.

Animal species of East Africa: 1 African wild dog (Lycaon pictus); 2 African elephant (Loxodonta africana); 3 Thomson's gazelle (Gazella thomsoni); 4 Cheetah (Acinonyx jubatus).

Map showing the distribution of the population in East Africa. The highest concentrations of people in this region are found around the Rift Valley lakes and in highland Ethiopia.

HOME TO THE EARLIEST KNOWN HUMANS, EAST AFRICA WITNESSED MANY MIGRATIONS AND POPULATION SHIFTS IN THE PAST. SINCE THE EARLY 20TH CENTURY, THE REGION'S POPULATION HAS GROWN DRAMATICALLY. MOST PEOPLE STILL LIVE ON THE LAND, THOUGH CITY DWELLING IS BECOMING EVER MORE COMMON.

RELIGION

East Africa has seen many religious movements over the centuries. Christianity arrived in highland Ethiopia in the early fourth century C.E., where it developed into a unique Orthodox Church, to which almost half the population still belong. Islam was introduced to the Red Sea and Somali coasts in the early seventh century, and spread down the East African coast. Today Eritrea, Djibouti, and Somalia are predominantly Muslim. The coasts of Kenya and Tanzania are also predominantly Muslim, along with around 45 percent of Ethiopia's population.

Inland Kenya and Tanzania, together with Uganda, Rwanda and Burundi, came under the influence of European Christian missionaries from the late 19th century on. Their success in converting people is reflected in the population breakdown by religion of these countries today: Rwanda's population is 93 percent Christian, Kenya's 78 percent, Burundi's 67 percent, Uganda's 66 percent, and Tanzania's 30 percent. Significant Asian immigration to each of these countries has greatly increased the

Map labels

ERITREA
Asmara.
SUDAN
Aksum.
.Mekele
Red Sea
Gondar.
DJIBOUTI
Lake Tana   ETHIOPIA   .Djibouti
Gulf of Aden
Dire Dawa.
Berbera
Blue Nile   Ethiopian   .Addis Ababa
.Hargeysa
Highlands   .Asela   SOMALIA
Horn of Africa
.Goba
White Nile
Shebelle River
Juba River
Lake Turkana
UGANDA   KENYA   .Mogadishu
Kampala.   .Eldoret
INDIAN OCEAN
.Kisumu   Tana River
.Kigali   .Nairobi   Kismaayo
RWANDA   Lake Victoria
BURUNDI   .Mwanza
.Bujumbura   Olduvai Gorge
Rift Valley
.Mombasa
Tanga.
.Dodoma   Zanzibar Island
Lake Tanganyika   TANZANIA
.Dar es Salaam
Rift Valley
.Mbeya
Lake Malawi
MALAWI   MOZAMBIQUE
Lilongwe.   Mozambique Channel

Population—people per 0.4 square miles (1 square km)
- 0–2
- 3–10
- 11–20
- 21–500
- 501–1000+

AFRO-ASIATIC LANGUAGE FAMILY

- Erythraic
  - Cushitic-Chadic
    - Chadic
    - Eastern Cushitic (e.g., Afar, Oromo, Somali peoples)
    - Southern Cushitic
    - Beja
  - Northern Afroasiatic
    - Berber
    - Egyptian
    - Others
    - Semitic
      - Arabic
      - Others
      - Amharic (e.g., Amhara, Falasha peoples)
- Omotic

percentages of Muslims, while small Hindu and Sikh populations live throughout the region, mainly in the large urban centers.

LANGUAGES

Two of East Africa's languages, Hadza and Sandawe, are "click" languages, which may be connected with the Khoisan languages of southern Africa. Both are spoken by hunter-gatherers or former hunter-gatherers in northwestern Tanzania.

Afro-Asiatic Languages

Afro-Asiatic languages are spoken throughout North and East Africa, Arabia, and the Near East. The Semitic subgroup of languages is well represented in East Africa today: Amhara is the dominant language of the Ethiopian highlands, while Tigrinya is widely spoken in northern Ethiopia and Eritrea. A second Afro-Asiatic subgroup, Cushitic-Chadic, is also widely spoken in Ethiopia, the Horn, and northern Kenya. It includes Oromo, Somali, Sidamo, Afar, and Rendille.

Nilotic Languages

Surmic-Nilotic languages form one branch of the Nilo-Saharan language family. Nilotic likely originated in the southern Sudan, from where a number of migrations, starting nearly 2,000 years ago, took it south into Kenya, Tanzania, and Uganda. Nilotic splits into three main branches; Western or River–Lake, spoken by the Luo of the Lake Victoria region; Southern or "Highland," spoken by the Kalenjin of western Kenya and the Datoga of Tanzania; and Eastern or "Plains," which further divides into the Atekar group, spoken by the Turkana, Teso and Karamojong, and the Maa group, spoken by the Samburu and Maasai.

Niger-Congo Languages

Bantu languages form one branch of the Niger-Congo language family. The original homeland of these languages is thought to

have been in southeastern Nigeria. Today Bantu speakers predominate in Tanzania, Kenya, Uganda, Rwanda, and Burundi. East African Bantu languages include Kirundi (Burundi), Kinyarwanda (Rwanda), Kinyoro and Luganda (Uganda), Kikuyu and Kikamba (Kenya), Kihaya and Kinyamwezi (Tanzania), and KiSwahili (spoken throughout the region).

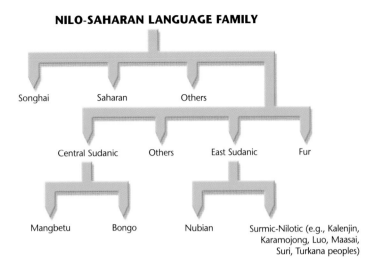

NILO-SAHARAN LANGUAGE FAMILY

Above, below, and opposite: Family trees of the Nilo-Saharan, Niger-Congo, and Afro-Asiatic language groups. The ethnic groups featured in this volume are listed in parentheses after the relevant language.

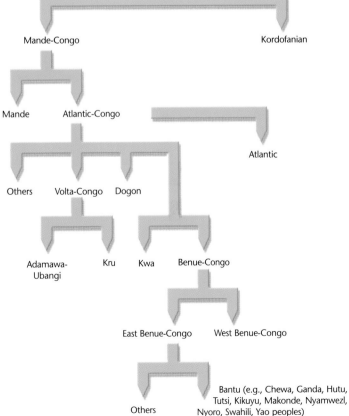

NIGER-CONGO LANGUAGE FAMILY

THE CULTURAL AND ARTISTIC MAKEUP OF EAST AFRICA IS BROAD AND VARIED. MOST ETHNIC GROUPS HAVE A LONG TRADITION OF MUSICMAKING, DANCE, AND STORYTELLING, WHILE MANY PRODUCE BEADWORK, BASKETRY, POTTERY, WOODWORK, LEATHERWORK, AND METALWORK.

MATERIAL CULTURE AND HANDICRAFTS

Historically a division of labor often took place between East African peoples who specialized in producing different items. Thus, some groups manufactured ceramics, others metalwork, and others basketry, which they then bartered with one another. In some societies, there were distinct castes of potters or metalworkers who lived apart from the rest of the community. These craftspeople, especially blacksmiths, were thought to be inspired by supernatural forces, and were viewed with a mixture of fear and respect.

Among many groups material objects took on a key role as symbols and regalia of kingship or other high office. Drums have particular importance among many Bantu chiefs and kings, as do stylized metal insignia, such as spears, anvils, staffs, and hammers. Dress and body adornment is often used to indicate an individual's position in society. Elaborate beadwork is used to convey group and personal status, while among the Mursi and Surma of southern Ethiopia a woman's status and beauty is indicated by the size of the ceramic plate inserted into her lower lip.

Precious items obtained through trade with the coast were especially sought after. The coastal Swahili made their own cloth, glass beads, ceramics, and metal items, which were traded inland along with highly valued items such as cowrie shells. The Swahili acquired great skill in stonemasonry, carving coral into elaborate shapes. Skilled stoneworking was also practiced in highland Ethiopia, creating the great stelae of Axum and the rock churches at Lalibela. Early Christian art of many types comes from Ethiopia.

Today artistic traditions are often applied to the tourist market. Beadwork jewelry and artifacts are now made for sale, along with a wide range of wood and soapstone carvings. Mass-produced carvings of animals and human figures are common, while the ornate and original wood carvings of the Makonde in Tanzania are highly prized. East Africa also has a thriving community of modern artists who fuse African and Western influences. Their works are exhibited in the major urban centers, such as Dar es Salaam, Kampala, Nairobi, and Addis Ababa.

An ancient inscribed stone in Ethiopia. Stone carving has long been associated with this mountainous country, which is home to impressive ancient rock monuments of the pre-Christian and Christian eras.

THE PERFORMING ARTS

Unlike the material arts, which have often been concentrated in the hands of specialists, the traditions of music, dance, and storytelling have usually been activities that the whole community engaged in, with men,

CHEWA

Totaling more than 1,500,000, the Chewa live in both Malawi and Zambia. This people dominated the politics of Malawi, with the Chewa leader Dr. Hastings Banda (1898–1997) exercising dictatorial rule in the country from 1964 to 1994. Their language, Chichewa, is one of Malawi's two official languages, along with English. Most of the Chewa are subsistence farmers—growing food for their own consumption—but some also cultivate tobacco as a cash crop. Beliefs that center on showing respect to the ancestors remain strong among the Chewa, and they believe in a creator god named Chiuta.

A Surma woman whose lower lip has been distended by wearing a lip-plate (though she does not have the plate in place here). Her body displays the finger-painted designs favored by the Surma.

SURMA

This people of southern Ethiopia combine livestock herding with cultivation, and place great value on their cattle. Surma women wear wooden or clay lip-plates, which gradually increase in size as they grow older. Some people believe that this custom may have started in the 19th century, as a way of deterring slavers from taking girls. Whatever its origin, the Surma today consider this practice as enhancing a woman's beauty. The Surma also decorate their bodies with intricate finger-painted designs. Another feature of Surma life that is attracting growing attention from the tourism industry is the *donga* stick fight, which young men armed with wooden staves perform to win a wife.

women, and children all taking part. Music and dance cannot generally be disengaged from the ceremonies and ritual activities of which they form a part. Throughout the region, music and dance play an important role in bringing the community together for rituals marking the seasons or a person's transition from one stage of life to another (rites of passage). Young men, for example of the Kikuyu and the Maasai in Kenya, are particularly well known for their dancing displays; these are designed both to demonstrate their fighting prowess and to attract sweethearts. Dances are often the occasion for forming lasting male–female relationships. Dances may be competitive, and also accompanied by recitals of the community's oral history. Nilotic livestock herders (pastoralists), in particular, are well known for their oral literature, which most

commonly sings the praises of their cattle. Competitive displays may also include feats of bravery in hunting, wrestling, and— as among the Surma of southern Ethiopia— impressive stick fights.

Ethiopia has a long tradition of flamboyant circuses that include displays of acrobatics and juggling. Today, regional circuses in Ethiopia have started a program of adopting young orphans, providing them with an education and nurturing their artistic talents. More recently traditional dances have been adapted into displays for tourists that can be seen in hotels, restaurants, and bars throughout the region. These entertainments often emphasize a broader trend in East African performing arts, of blending African and Western styles. In particular, the thriving East African popular music scene has been greatly influenced by Central African and North American styles.

Theater is also popular and widespread. Drawing on traditions of satire and mimicry, East African theater is increasingly used as a forum for tackling difficult issues such as HIV/AIDS and contraception, women's rights, and interethnic conflict.

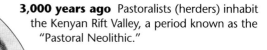

6 million years ago Early possible hominid *Orrorin tugenensis*, exists in Tugen Hills in Kenya.

4.5 million years ago First bipedal hominid *Ardipithecus ramidus*, living in southern Ethiopia.

3.5 million years ago *Australopithecus afarensis* is living throughout East Africa. These early hominids include the famous near-complete skeleton from Hadar, northeast Ethiopia, nicknamed "Lucy," and footprints found fossilized in volcanic ash at Laetoli in northern Tanzania.

2.5 million years ago The earliest stone tool industry appears. Around the same time a new hominid species named *Homo habilis* appears throughout East Africa .

1.8 million years ago Emergence of *Homo ergaster*, the first hominid to leave Africa. Specimens include the famous "Turkana boy."

150,000 years ago Earliest known modern humans are living at Herto, southern Ethiopia.

30,000 years ago First possible evidence of rock art in East Africa, from Irangi Hills in north-central Tanzania.

4,000 years ago First evidence of domestic livestock in East Africa.

East Africa is where humankind originated. This is a reconstruction of an early hominid.

3,000 years ago Pastoralists (herders) inhabit the Kenyan Rift Valley, a period known as the "Pastoral Neolithic."

2,500 years ago First Bantu-speaking farmers settle in the East African lakes region. First clear evidence of agriculture and ironworking. Settlers from Saba (Yemen, Arabia) found a state just north of Axum, Ethiopia.

2,000 years ago Bantu speakers reach the East African coast and Nilotic herders and crop growers move south into Kenya.

1–100 C.E. Development of Axumite civilization in Ethiopia. Greco-Roman texts, such as the *Periplus of the Erythraean Sea*, bear witness to limited Eurasian contact with the coast of East Africa and Axum.

c.330 Christianity is introduced to Axumite Ethiopia.

c.650 Establishment of Sultanate of Adel by Arab tribes on the coasts of Eritrea, Djibouti, and Somalia.

c.700 Decline of Axumite civilization.

c.780 In the wake of trade with visiting Arabian and Persian merchants, the earliest known mosque in East Africa is constructed at Shanga on Kenya's Lamu archipelago.

900–1000 First urban stone town built at Kilwa Island in southern Tanzania.

1000–1400 Kingdoms of Rwanda and Burundi established under Tutsi monarchs (mwami). Foundation of Bunyoro–Kitara kingdom, centered on Ntusi in Western Uganda.

1137–1270 Founding of Zagwe Dynasty in Ethiopia and construction of the famous rock-hewn churches of Lalibela.

1270 Dynasty of "Solomonic" kings established by Yekuno Amlak in Ethiopia; they claim descent from King Solomon and the Queen of Sheba (Saba).

c.1300 Construction of the great palace of Husuni Kubwa at Kilwa Kisiwani.

Kilwa Kisiwani, a small island off the coast of southern Tanzania, became a major trading port serving the Indian Ocean and African interior. Impressive stone buildings were erected at this site, including a Great Mosque and sultans' palaces. These are the ruins of the 14th-century palace of Husuni Kubwa.

1331 Arab traveler Ibn Battuta travels to the Swahili coast and states that the inhabitants of Kilwa were "Zanj, jet-black in color, and with tattoo marks on their faces."

c.1350–1400 Decline of Kilwa, while towns at Mombasa and Malindi flourish.

c.1450 Construction of impressive agricultural ruins at Engaruka in north-west Tanzania.

1498–99 Portuguese navigator Vasco de Gama rounds the Cape of Good Hope, stopping at the Swahili town of Malindi en route to India.

1500–1550 Muslim–Christian wars in Ethiopia. Ottoman Empire annexes Eritrea.

1500–1600 Portuguese take control of Swahili coast, building forts at Kilwa and Mombasa. Corn is introduced to East Africa from the Americas. Disintegration of the Sultanate of Adel. Southward migration of Nilotic Luo into Uganda. Development of Buganda and Ankole Kingdoms in Uganda and Karagwe Kingdom in northwest Tanzania.

1550–1750 Expansion of the Oromo (Galla) northward into Ethiopia from Kenya.

c.1600 Rwandan rulers begin a gradual process of expansion and consolidation. Their capital is established at Nyanza.

1600–1700 Maasai push southward from Turkana region into present-day locations. Around this time the modern Kalenjin groups form in Kenya.

1606 Omani Arabs take Pemba from the Portuguese and begin their conquest of the East African coast.

1636 Reformation of a strong Christian state in highland Ethiopia based at Gondar.

1698 The Omanis take the last Portuguese stronghold in East Africa, at Fort Jesus in Mombasa.

c.1700 Impressive large-scale, indigenous irrigation systems are constructed at Marakwet along the western escarpment of the Rift Valley north of Baringo. Decline of the Bunyoro Kingdom in Uganda, Buganda rises to prominence.

The Scottish missionary David Livingstone explored East and Central Africa from the 1860s onward with the aim spreading Christianity.

1798 Britain and Oman establish a commercial trade treaty over the East African coast.

1832 Sultan of Oman moves his capital to Zanzibar. Arab slave traders from the north and the coast push deep inland reaching the lakes region.

1855 Ethiopian kingdom of Gondar dissolves into small regional fiefdoms.

1857 European exploration of East Africa begins in earnest with Burton and Speke's two year journey to Tanganyika and Victoria Nyanza. This is followed by Speke and Grant in 1860–63 who visit Bunyoro and Buganda, Baker in 1863–73, Livingstone in 1866–73, and Stanley 1871–77.

1875 Egypt occupies towns on the Somali coast. French gain a foothold in the territory later known as Djibouti.

1885 The Berlin Conference sees Africa divided among the European powers. The Italians establish themselves on the coast of present-day Eritrea.

1887 Britain declares a protectorate over northern Somalia.

1888 British East Africa Company begins conquest of Kenya, building trading forts from Mombasa inland.

1888–1907 German conquest of mainland Tanganyika.

1889 Emperor Menelik II ascends the Ethiopian throne and creates the modern kingdom of Ethiopia. Eritrea is occupied by the Italians, who also establish a Somali protectorate to the south of British Somaliland.

1890 Zanzibar becomes British protectorate and the slave trade is officially ended.

1892 The British East Africa Company sign a treaty with the Kabaka of Buganda and in 1894 Buganda becomes a British protectorate. Running battles occur between British forces and the Bunyoro King Kabalega.

1894–98 Rwanda and Burundi incorporated into German East Africa.

1895–1901 The Mombasa–Uganda railroad is built. British settlers begin to populate the Kenyan highlands.

1896 Menelik II's Ethiopian army defeats invading Italian forces at the Battle of Adowa.

1913 Death of Menelik II in Ethiopia and accession of his grandson Iyasu.

1914–18 German forces in Tanganyika wage a guerrilla war against British East Africa during World War I.

Italian troops assemble in Eritrea in 1935 in preparation for the invasion of Abyssinia (Ethiopia). Italian Fascist dictator Mussolini's forces used poison gas against the Ethiopians.

Ras Tafari (Crown Prince) Haile Selassie was crowned emperor of Ethiopia in 1930. His rule was interrupted by Italian occupation, but lasted until 1974, when he was deposed and later murdered.

1916 Belgian invasion of Rwanda–Burundi. Belgian control is officially sanctioned under a League of Nations mandate in 1919.

1918 End of World War I sees Tanganyika become a British mandated territory (colony).

1921 Deposition of Iyasu in Ethiopia. Menelik II's daughter, Zewditu, is proclaimed empress. Haile Selassie (the son of Menelik's cousin) is proclaimed prince regent.

1930 Zewditu dies and Haile Selassie is crowned emperor of Ethiopia. In Rwanda and Burundi the Catholic Church is entrusted with full responsibility for the educational system.

1935 Italian conquest of Ethiopia. Ethiopia, Somalia, and Eritrea are unified to create Italian East Africa. In Rwanda and Burundi the Belgian administration confirms a three-part ethnic division (Twa, Hutu, Tutsi) by introducing ethnic identity cards.

1939 Start of World War II. Many East Africans are called to serve in the King's African Rifles, a British army unit.

1940 Italians occupy British Somaliland. Britain regains the territory in 1941 and occupies Italian Somaliland and Italian Eritrea.

1941 British and Ethiopian forces liberate Addis Ababa from Italian occupation.

1946 Djibouti becomes an overseas territory within the French Union with its own legislature and representation in the French parliament.

1952 Start of Mau Mau uprisings in Kenya. British respond harshly, detaining people without trial in concentration camps. Under UN mandate, British-administered Eritrea becomes federated with Ethiopia.

1956 Mau Mau ends with execution of guerrilla leader Dedan Kimathi.

1957 Presentation of Hutu Manifesto in Rwanda and formation of Hutu political parties supported by the Catholic Church.

1959 The run-up to independence sees the first Hutu and Tutsi clashes in Rwanda and Burundi. The Belgian administration begins replacing minority Tutsi officials with majority Hutus.

1960 British and Italian Somaliland gain independence and merge to form the united republic of Somalia. Lancaster House Conference in London sees African representatives gain majority in the Kenyan Legislative Council. Kikuyu–Luo dominated Kenyan African National Union (KANU) and more moderate Kenyan African Democratic Union (KADU) are formed.

1961 Hastily arranged elections in Rwanda see the Hutu majority gain control and the country proclaimed a republic. Anti-Tutsi violence escalates and thousands leave the country, many fleeing into neighboring Congo and Uganda. Grégoire Kayibanda becomes the first president. In Tanzania the Tanganyika African National Union (TANU) wins the majority of seats of the Legislative Council and independence is granted with TANU leader Kambarage Nyerere as the country's first president.

1962 Uganda gains independence under prime minister Milton Obote. Burundi is given independence as a monarchy under Tutsi King Mwambutsa IV. Ethiopia annexes Eritrea, sparking a long independence war.

1963 Zanzibar and Kenya both gain independence.

1964 War between Ethiopia and Somalia. Kenya becomes a republic with Jomo Kenyatta as the first president.

1964 Sultan of Zanzibar is overthrown in bloody revolution, and Zanzibar unites with newly independent Tanganyika, forming the united republic of Tanzania.

1965 In Burundi Mwambutsa's refusal to appoint a Hutu prime minister sparks riots and an attempted coup.

1966 In Uganda, Obote scraps the independence constitution, deposes Kabaka Mutesa II as head of state, and appoints himself president for life. A second coup in Burundi is successful and its leader Michel Micombero declares himself president.

Leaders of the Mau Mau in Kenya. This major rebellion against British colonial rule was led by the Kikuyu. Atrocities were committed by both sides, and the British interned many Kenyans, including the future president Jomo Kenyatta.

1967 Tanzanian president Julius Nyerere makes the Arusha Declaration announcing his vision for "African Socialism." His ideals translate into "villagization," a program of forced resettlement. These policies are economically disastrous, but foreign aid brings great improvements in education and health care. Creation of the East African Community between Uganda, Kenya and Tanzania.

1969–70 Muhammad Siad Barre assumes power in Somalia after a military coup. He declares Somalia a socialist state and nationalizes most of the economy.

1971 Head of the Ugandan army, Idi Amin, stages a coup and declares himself president.

1972 In Uganda Amin expels all Asians and "Africanizes" their businesses. He begins a reign of terror, executing all political and intellectual opponents.

1973 In the face of increasing corruption and extreme anti-Tutsi measures in Rwanda, President Kayibanda is toppled in a military coup. He is replaced by Major General Juvenal Habyarimana.

1974 Massive popular uprisings in Ethiopia depose Haile Selassie. The Provisional Military Administrative Council (popularly known as the Derg) under Colonel Mengistu Haile Mariam seizes power. Ethiopia is declared a socialist state and in 1975 the aging Haile Selassie is murdered.

1976 In Burundi President Micombero is deposed in a military coup and replaced by Jean-Baptiste Bagaza.

Idi Amin seized power in a coup in Uganda in 1971. His rule was extremely cruel, and he showed signs of increasing mental instability. He was deposed in 1979 by Tanzanian forces.

1977 Somali invasion of Ethiopia is repelled. French Somaliland becomes independent and is renamed Djibouti. The East African Community collapses.

1978 Ugandan president Idi Amin declares war on Tanzania. The following year a newly formed Tanzanian army takes Kampala and drives him into exile. On the death of Kenyatta, Tugen vice-president Daniel Arap Moi becomes Kenya's second president.

1980 Uganda's first election since 1962 sees the Ugandan Peoples Congress (UPC) win a rigged vote. Milton Obote returns to power. Yoweri Museveni establishes the National Resistance Movement and begins a guerrilla war against the Obote regime. The Rwandan Alliance for National Unity (RANU) is established among Rwandan refugees in western Uganda.

1981 Djibouti becomes a one-party state with the People's Progress Assembly as the sole party.

1982 In Kenya constitutional amendments ban all political parties other than KANU and there is a failed coup by the Kenyan Air Force.

1984–85 Massive famine in Ethiopia sparks worldwide appeals for aid, including the famous "Band Aid" appeal and "Live Aid" concerts.

1985 Increasingly disillusioned with the failure of his economic policies, Nyerere resigns from the Tanzanian presidency. He is replaced by Ali Hassan Mwinyi, who makes sweeping economic reforms.

1986 Yoweri Museveni's National Resistance Army (supported by RANU) overthrows Obote and assumes power in Uganda.

1987–88 Military coup in Burundi sees Tutsi Pierre Buyoya take the presidency. Thousands of Hutus are massacred by Tutsi and a flood of refugees move into southern Rwanda.

1989 Formation of Ethiopian People's Revolutionary Democratic Front (EPRDF).

1990 Rwandan Patriotic Front (RPF) invade northern Rwanda from Uganda but are repelled. President Habyarimana agrees to bring in multiparty politics and abolish ethnic identity cards, but the army trains Interahamwe ("those who stand together") militias.

1991 Facing the EPRDF at home and the Eritrean People's Liberation Front (EPLF) in Eritrea, Mengistu flees Ethiopia. Independence is given to Eritrea. In Somalia opposition clans oust Barre. Somalia declines into civil conflict and Somaliland (the area formerly called British Somaliland) declares independence.

1992 U.S. marines land near Mogadishu in Somalia ahead of a UN peacekeeping force. After suffering losses and failing in their peace-keeping mission the marines and the UN forces withdraw in 1995. In Kenya donor nations withdraw funding, forcing Moi to reestablish multiparty elections. However, with electoral corruption and a split opposition KANU wins the elections and Moi retains the presidency. Djibouti adopts a multiparty system.

1993 Under increasing RPF attacks, led by Major Paul Kagame, the Arusha Agreement over Rwanda is signed. The Agreement commits the Rwandan government to major reforms, but, being unpalatable to both Hutu and Tutsi hardliners, they are not implemented. In Burundi Melchior Ndadaye, a Hutu, beats Buyoya in the country's first presidential election and becomes the first Hutu president. Just months later he is assassinated.

1994 A plane carrying Rwanda's president Habyarimana and Burundi's new Hutu president Cyprien Ntaryamira crashes, killing both men. Within hours the Rwandan military and the Interahamwe begin slaughtering Tutsi and moderate Hutu. As the international community fails to act, three months of terror end with nearly one million people murdered. The RPF captures Kigali and end the genocide.

1995 Tanzania's first multiparty elections see Benjamin Mkapa elected to the mainland presidency, but violent uprisings break out on Zanzibar.

Ethiopians at a refugee camp in 1984. The plight of Ethiopia touched many in the developed world. Insufficient rainfall that made the harvest fail first sparked the crisis, which was made worse by poverty and ongoing military conflict in the region.

1996 Tutsi Pierre Buyoya stages a second coup in Burundi, deposing temporary president Sylvestre Ntibantunganya, and suspending the constitution. Burundi dissolves into a factional civil war. Popular Ugandan president Yoweri Museveni wins the country's first presidential election since 1986.

1997 In Kenya KANU again wins elections amid claims of vote rigging and a hopelessly divided opposition. However, Mwai Kibaki's Democratic Party do well in Kikuyuland, taking many KANU seats and Daniel Arap Moi announces that this will be his final term as president.

1998 U.S. embassies in Nairobi and Dar es Salaam are bombed by affiliates of al-Qaeda.

1998–2000 A border dispute leads to war between Ethiopia and Eritrea.

1999 Ismael Omar Gelleh elected president of Djibouti.

2000 The EPRDF and Meles Zenawi win elections in Ethiopia. Paul Kagame becomes the fifth president of Rwanda; he is again reelected in 2003. Elections in Tanzania see a repeat of 1995 with Mkapa reelected but widespread violence on Zanzibar.

2001 Transitional power sharing government established in Burundi. The main Hutu rebels refuse to sign cease-fire. In Eritrea all nongovernmental press organizations are outlawed. The East African Union between Kenya, Uganda, and Tanzania is reinstated.

2002 Kenya's President Moi retires; Mwai Kibaki wins presidential election as head of Kenya's new National Rainbow Coalition (NARC). Rwanda re-creates a system of traditional courts known as the "Gacaca" to promote reconciliation among people accused of lesser crimes during the genocide. In strategic Djibouti, 900 U.S. troops establish a military base in support of the "war on terror."

2003 Major Hutu rebel groups are eventually incorporated into the Burundi government ending the civil war. Democratic presidential elections in breakaway Somaliland see Dahir Riyale Kahin elected, but the territory still lacks international recognition.

2004 Somali warlords and politicians agree to establish a new government. A transitional Somali government is formed in exile in Kenya and Abdullahi Yusuf elected president. Indian Ocean tsunami hits the Somali coast, killing hundreds and displacing thousands.

2005 Meles Zenawi and the EPRDF win another election in Ethiopia. In Burundi, leader of the major Hutu rebel group, Forces for the Defense of Democracy (FDD), is elected president. World Food Program brings aid to drought-hit Eritrea. Kenyan voters reject new constitution put forward by President Mwai Kibaki.

AFAR

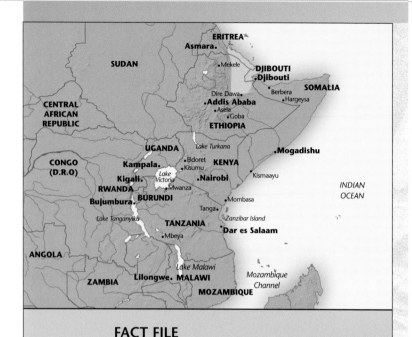

FACT FILE

Population	Around 3.4 million Afar, split between Ethiopia (3 million), Djibouti (180,000), and Eritrea (182,000)
Religion	Sunni Islam, Christianity, preexisting beliefs
Language	The Afar language is Lowland Eastern Cushitic. Arabic is also spoken and a little French in Djibouti.

TIMELINE

10th century	Afar begin moving down from the highlands into lowland regions, and to convert to Islam.
late 16th century	Afar fight for Ahmad Gran, the emir of Harar, who tries to create a Muslim empire in the Ethiopian Highlands.
19th century	Afar fight for kingdom of Adel against Christian Amhara.
1875	Egypt and France colonize coastal regions.
1889	Emperor Menelik II incorporates most Afar into the kingdom of Ethiopia. Eritrea occupied by Italy.
1935–41	Italians overrun the region and create Italian East Africa; later driven out by British and Ethiopian forces.
1967	French Somaliland renamed French Territory of the Afars and Issas (independence as Djibouti in 1977).
1974	Marxist Colonel Mengistu seizes power in Ethiopia.
1975	Formation of the Afar Liberation Front in Ethiopia.
1989	Djibouti becomes a one-party state.
1991	Mengistu flees Ethiopia. Eritrea wins independence (in 1993 referendum). Afar revolt starts in Djibouti.
2005	The World Food Program moves into Eritrea to help after a series of droughts.

THE AFAR LIVE IN THE ARID, INHOSPITABLE DANAKIL DESERT BORDERING THE RED SEA COAST OF ERITREA AND DJIBOUTI, AND EXTENDING INTO THE NORTHEAST OF LANDLOCKED ETHIOPIA. FOR A LONG TIME, THEY HAVE BEEN ENGAGED IN A STRUGGLE FOR SELF-DETERMINATION.

HISTORY

The origins of the Afar are not well known. They are Lowland Eastern Cushitic speakers who are closely related to the Saho, Somali, and Oromo peoples. Over the last 1,000 years they appear to have moved gradually down from the Ethiopian Highlands into the Eastern lowlands of Ethiopia, Eritrea, and Djibouti. During the course of this slow migration, they became nomadic livestock herders, a lifestyle that is appropriate to the incredibly harsh, arid environment of the Danakil desert. The Afar clans mostly claim Arab descent, although this is probably a mythical tradition that developed as a means of enhancing their status and authority. The wealth of linguistic and cultural similarities between the Afar and other Eastern Cushitic peoples testifies to their African origin. Over the centuries the Afar have also been active in many conflicts between lowland Islamic leaders and Christian highland Ethiopia.

In the mid-1970s the Afar Liberation Front (ALF) was formed and began guerrilla activities in Ethiopia to press for greater autonomy. The creation of the Autonomous Region of Assab (now in Eritrea) partly addressed this issue, but low level conflict continued until the early 1990s when

An Afar man. The Afar are renowned for their pride and resilience, and have fought a series of wars against both regional and foreign powers that have attempted to rule their region.

A camel caravan of the Afar crosses the rocky desert terrain of the Danakil Depression, carrying salt for trading at the markets of Senbete and Bati in inland Ethiopia.

Ethiopia's new federal constitution saw real power devolved to the regions, including Afar. Parallel, but less violent, Afar independence movements were also established in Djibouti.

SOCIETY AND DAILY LIFE

In common with other pastoralist peoples, there has been a growing trend over recent decades for the Afar to abandon their nomadic way of life in search of work. Even so, most Afar still remain nomadic pastoralists, herding sheep, goats, cattle, and camels. They live mainly on a diet of milk and meat, which they supplement by selling salt dug from the coastal desert. During the dry season most Afar relocate to the banks of the Awash River where there is good grazing. With the arrival of the November rains they move to higher ground to avoid flooding and mosquitoes. The Afar live in tent houses known as *ari*, which are made of sticks covered with mats and skins. Houses are arranged into *burra*, or camps, comprising two or more *ari*. The women are mainly responsible for these camps, while the men's task is to tend after the livestock.

The Afar are organized into four patrilineal clans, or sections. These are further divided into classes, of which the *asaimara* ("reds") are the dominant group, with the *adoimara* ("whites") forming a working class. Politically the Afar are a loose confederation of four sultanates. However, sultans are not hereditary, but are chosen by general agreement from alternating segments of each of the four sections.

CULTURE AND RELIGION

The Afar are predominantly Sunni Muslims, with just 3 percent following Christianity. While conversion to Islam likely began in the 10th century or earlier, many pre-Islamic beliefs, ceremonies, and festivals remain important. In particular, some rural Afar women still walk around bare-breasted, which is unusual for devout Muslims. As is common among Arabian peoples, marriage preferences are for the first cousin, a system that ensures bridewealth payments remain within the clan. Circumcision is practiced on both boys and girls. Boys are supposed to undergo the operation without displaying weakness, while female circumcision, or female genital mutilation (FGM), involves the controversial practice of infibulation, or sewing together and damaging the vulva.

SEE ALSO: *Amhara; Islam; Music and musical instruments.*

THE DANAKIL DEPRESSION

The Danakil Depression is home to the Afar. It is the lowest point in Africa, some 492 feet (150 m) below sea level, and has some of the highest temperatures in the world. Rainfall here is extremely low, only 4–8 inches (100–200 mm) per year, and life is only possible thanks to the Awash River, which runs northeastward through the region. About 80 miles (130 km) from the Red Sea the Awash itself runs into a chain of salt lakes where steady evaporation occurs. The Afar maintain a fragile balance with this ecosystem and have been instrumental in the survival of the last viable population of the African wild ass. The depression is also known as one of the "cradles of humankind"; the skeleton of an early hominid (human predecessor) nicknamed "Lucy," was found here in 1974.

AFRICAN-LANGUAGE LITERATURE

MAJOR WORKS AND THEIR AUTHORS

Title	Date	Author	Country/Language
Basekabaka be Buganda (The Kings of Buganda);	1894	Apolo Kagwa	Uganda/Luganda
Engero za Buganda (Ugandan Folk Stories)	1927		
Utendi wa Liyongo Fumo (Songs of Liyongo Fumo)	1913	Muhammad bin Abubakar	Kenya/Swahili
Pamba la lugha (Beauty of the Language)	1948	Shabaan Robert	Tanzania/Swahili
Sigend Luo mu duogo chuny (Merry Luo Stories)	1951	S. Malo	Kenya/Luo
Muddu Awlulira (The Obedient Servant)	1953	Michael Nsimbi	Uganda/Luganda
Lak tar miyo kinyero wi lobo (If Your Teeth are White, Laugh)	1953	Okot P'Bitek	Uganda/Luo
Abagabe b'Ankole (The Kings of Ankole)	1955	A. Katate & L. Kamungungunu	Uganda/ Runyankore
Kikonyogo (Unexpected Luck)	1961	Christopher Musisi	Uganda/Luganda
Lacan ma kwo pe kinyero (Every Dog Has Its Day)	1961	J. Ocitti	Uganda/Luo
Kutheea kuma yayayanil (From the Sky)	1962	Thomas Ngotho	Kenya/Luo
Bururi Wa Embu (History of the Embu People)	1962	D. Michuki	Kenya/Gikuyu
Ha munwa gw'ekituuro (At the Point of Death)	c.1963	Timothy Bazarrabusa	Uganda/Lunyoro
Jamhuri ya Tanzania (History of Tanzania)	1968	R. Maruka	Tanzania/Swahili
Rosa mistika (Mystic Rose)	1971	Euphrase Kezilahabi	Tanzania/Swahili
Mashetani (Devils)	1971	Micere Mugo	Tanzania/Swahili
Oluyimba Lwa Wankoko (Song of the Cock)	1977	Byron Kawadwa	Uganda/Luganda
Cautaani Mutharaba-Ini (Devil on the Cross)	1980	Ngugi wa Thiong'o	Kenya/Gikuyu
Matigari ma Njuruungi (Matigari)	1986		
Murogi wa Kagogo (Wizard of the Crow)	2004		

THE AFRICAN-LANGUAGE LITERATURES OF EAST AFRICA ARE AMONG THE OLDEST AND MOST DIVERSE ON THE CONTINENT. THEY HAVE BEEN INFLUENCED BY THE LITERARY TRADITIONS BROUGHT BY SUCCESSIVE WAVES OF MIGRANTS. YET LITERATURE IN AFRICAN LANGUAGES IS UNDER THREAT FROM THE POPULARITY OF WRITING IN ENGLISH AND FRENCH.

HISTORY

The earliest East African written literature was exclusive to religious specialists, and the first texts were on sacred or devotional themes. However, as literary knowledge and writing skills spread, written literature gradually also became associated with political authority. Kings or chiefs would sometimes employ literary specialists to write down praise poems (which would formerly have been delivered orally).

After European missionaries began to arrive in East Africa in the early 16th century, written texts once again became a preserve of religious elites. Throughout the colonial period, literature in indigenous languages was dominated by Christian works that had been translated from European languages into a variety of East African tongues. The picture changed once more in the period immediately before and after independence, as African scholars found their voice and developed new forms of writing in history, fiction, and social commentary.

THE LITERATURES OF ETHIOPIA

The art of writing was introduced to highland Ethiopia and Eritrea from Arabia in the fourth century B.C.E. Texts of this time used an alphabet that was gradually adapted

THE LEGEND OF LIYONGO FUMO

The Legend of Liyongo Fumo was first written down by Muhammad bin Abubakar in 1913. However, it had existed as an oral poem for at least five hundred years before that. The legend is a typical Swahili epic, telling the tragic story of the hero Liyongo. Like the ancient Greek hero Achilles, Liyongo is a superhuman figure who wins prestige and power through his prowess on the battlefield. Liyongo is the rightful heir to the throne of Lamu Island but never takes possession of his kingdom. His envious brother discovers that Liyongo (like Achilles, with his vulnerable heel) can be hurt by just one weapon: a copper knife. Accordingly, his brother and his cowardly son conspire to murder the hero.

to the local Ethiopic language to form a written language known as Ge'ez. In the fourth century C.E., King Ezana of the ancient Ethiopian kingdom of Axum was converted to Christianity by a monk named Frumentius from Alexandria, Egypt. Ge'ez literature flourished during the Christian era, as the clergy under the leadership of missionaries from Syria translated the Bible and other religious texts.

By around 1200 Ge'ez had largely died out as a spoken language and been replaced by Amharic. Yet the Christian clergy preserved it as a language of literature and worship. Indeed, the period between 1270 and 1543 is often called the "golden age" of Ge'ez literature. Over that period, the body of religious texts increased greatly, mostly through the additon of works translated from European languages. In addition, a

THE KEBRA NAGAST

It is not known exactly, when, where, and by whom the *Kebra Nagast* ("Book of the Glory of the Kings of Ethiopia") was written. It was probably begun by scribes at the royal court in the city of Axum, shortly after it was made the capital of Ethiopia by King Yekuno Amlak in 1270. Written in a form of Ge'ez, the book is a collection of histories, legends, and oral traditions relating to the origin of the royal house of Ethiopia. Its central section describes the investiture of Menelik—the first King of Ethiopia—by his father, King Solomon. Today, Ethiopian Christians and Rastafarians still revere the Kebra Nagast as a sacred text, with many seeing it not as legend but as the ultimate authority on Ethiopian history.

new group of court scribes began to produce praise poems in honor of the monarch and his armies. The most famous of these texts is the *Kebra Nagast* (see box feature). However, the elite nature of Ge'ez writing eventually led to its downfall. From the 17th century onward, Jesuit and Protestant missionaries began arriving in the region. Alarmed that religious texts in Ge'ez could not be read by most of the population, the new missionaries set about transcribing the same texts into Amharic, using the Roman script. Because of the popular accessibility of these new works, over time, they almost entirely replaced Ge'ez writings. Throughout the 19th and 20th centuries, a new, popular Amharic literature developed, embracing works of prose, poetry, and drama.

SWAHILI LITERATURE

The Swahili coast has a long tradition of epic oral poetry stretching back several millennia. Like the earliest European epics, these poems recounted legends of heroic warriors and their quest for fame and fortune. Yet it was not until the 14th century—more than a thousand years after literacy had first arrived in Ethiopia—that writing was introduced to the Swahili coast. At that time, as part of an intense wave of conversion to Islam, traders from the Middle East introduced Arabic script. Written mostly in the Arabic language, the earliest books were translations of the Quran and the Muslim hadith (laws and practices) and other religious texts. However, it was another four centuries before any books were written in Swahili. Once again, most of these texts were of a religious nature.

The new Swahili literature found a unique way of presenting Islamic themes, by using the ancient heroic epics as storytelling vehicles. For example, the life and struggles of the Prophet Muhammad were recast using all the familiar elements of the oral legends. As with Ge'ez, over time, more secular (nonreligious) forms of writing also began to emerge, especially political texts. Unlike Ethiopian literature, Swahili political writing did not praise leaders but instead criticized them for ignoring the plight of common people. The early development of this type of Swahili literature was a key influence on the later writing of works of social commentary and political protest during the period of direct European rule.

19TH AND 20TH CENTURIES

The advent of direct European colonialism in East Africa in the late 19th century had a huge impact upon the development of African-language literature throughout East Africa. On the one hand, it led to all earlier forms of writing being replaced by the standard Roman script. Thus, from the 1890s onward, most Swahili texts were no longer written in Arabic, but instead in the Roman alphabet (this shift mirrored earlier developments in Ethiopia). On the other hand, it led to various other oral traditions being written down for the first time. One such tradition was Somali oral poetry. Despite its long and rich history, and its very vivid and poetic style, Somali poetry was not committed to paper until the final decade of the 19th century.

The introduction of Western education helped spread literacy throughout the region. This in turn led to the production of more, and more varied, literature. The earliest agents of Western education were Christian missionaries, and so most of the early works from this period were concerned with religious matters. However, as education became more widespread, and African-language authors became more familiar with European styles, new forms of writing also emerged: history, political drama, critical poetry, and so on.

The East African Literature Bureau was established by the British colonial authorities in the late 1940s to stimulate publications in

TANZANIAN LANGUAGE POLICY

Tanzania is the only East African country that has continued to produce a steady output of African-language literature after independence. This is largely the result of government policy since 1966, which has aimed at establishing Swahili as the national language. The deliberate promotion of Swahili has been at the expense of the colonial language, English. For example, when Tanzania experienced paper shortages between 1971 and 1974, priority supplies were given to publishers and printers that produced literature and textbooks in Swahili. As a result, over the last 30 years Swahili literature has thrived in Tanzania, while African-language publishing has been in decline elsewhere.

African languages. In the years immediately before and after independence, nationalist history and political satire became increasingly important literary forms. Nowhere was this more apparent than in Kenya, where writers built on the long local tradition of writing as a form of political protest to write devastating criticisms of the corruption of the postcolonial state. When Ngugi wa Thiong'o (b.1938) wrote a play in Kikuyu in the late 1970s attacking the regime, he was imprisoned and dismissed from his post at the University of Nairobi. The situation in Uganda during the brutal regime of Idi Amin (1971–79) was even worse. The country's leading playwright Byron Kawadwa, who wrote in the Luganda language, was dragged from the theater and murdered for writing a critical play in 1977.

Despite the powerful critical voice of African-language literature, it has steadily lost ground in the postcolonial period. From the mid-1960s on, many publishers urged authors to write in English rather than their native language to increase their readership and sales. The only exception to this general rule was Tanzania, where the official policy of promoting Swahili as an inclusive national language has produced a steady stream of literary works in that language.

SEE ALSO: *Amhara; Christianity; English-language literature; Falasha; Ganda; Islam; Luo; Oral literature.*

FACT FILE

Population	Approximately 23 million, all in Ethiopia
Religion	Ethiopian Orthodox Christianity
Language	Amharic is a Semitic language, most closely related to Tigrinya but also to Hebrew and Arabic.

TIMELINE

c.330	Introduction of Christianity to Axumite Ethiopia.
1270	Amhara "Solomonic" dynasty established in Ethiopia.
1550–1750	Oromo expansion north sparks conflict with Amhara.
1636	Establishment of the Ethiopian capital at Gondar.
1855	Gondar-based empire begins to break up.
1889	Emperor Menelik II comes to power and consolidates the modern kingdom of Ethiopia.
1896	Menelik's army defeats the Italians at battle of Adowa.
1913	Menelik II dies and is succeeded by his grandson Iyasu.
1930	Ras Tafari (Crown Prince) is made Emperor Haile Selassie I.
1935	Italian forces annex Ethiopia, Somalia, and Eritrea.
1941	British and Ethiopian army expels Italian forces.
1974	Haile Selassie overthrown and later murdered by communist regime of Colonel Mengistu Haile Mariam.
1991	Mengistu driven out and a new government is formed under Meles Zenawi.
1994	A new federal constitution establishes Amhara as one of nine federal regions.
2005	Axum stele, looted by Italy in 1937, returns to Ethiopia.

I N ANCIENT TIMES, THE AMHARA RULED THE HIGHLANDS OF ETHIOPIA AND CLAIMED DESCENT FROM THE BIBLICAL KING SOLOMON. THEY STILL DOMINATE ETHIOPIAN POLITICAL AND ECONOMIC LIFE.

HISTORY

The Amhara are thought to be the descendants of Semitic peoples from what is now Yemen who crossed the Red Sea and settled parts of Ethiopia from the sixth century B.C.E. on. There they mingled with the native Cushitic people of the Ethiopian highlands. The Amhara themselves trace their origins to the legendary King Menelik I, legendary son of King Solomon of Israel and the Queen of Sheba. Menelik is supposed to have founded the ancient kingdom of Axum in around 960 B.C.E. However, historical records date the emergence of this kingdom to the first century C.E.

The Axumite kingdom gradually came to be dominated by the Amhara but declined following the spread of Islam from 640 on. Its successor state Ethiopia, founded in around 1100, was also under their control by 1270, when King Yekuno Amlak established the Amhara "Solomonic" dynasty that lasted until Haile Selassie's overthrow in 1974.

SOCIETY AND DAILY LIFE

Most Amhara are farmers cultivating barley, corn, millet, wheat, and teff (see box feature) along with beans, peppers, and other vegetables. Until the Ethiopian revolution of 1974 the Amhara elite widened their control through a feudal system of land tenure known as *gebbar*. This system allowed peasants to choose what crops to grow but required them to give a percentage of their produce (*gult*) to the feudal lord. There was little impetus for improvement or

TEFF—A VERSATILE CEREAL

Teff (*Eragrostis tef*) is a species of grass native to North Africa that was domesticated as a cereal crop more than 3,000 years ago. It is very nutritious and contains high levels of protein, iron, and vitamins. Despite the fact that its small grain size makes it relatively uneconomic to grow and harvest, teff remains an important staple crop for the Amhara and others throughout much of highland Ethiopia. It is principally used to make a large, fermented flatbread called *injera*, which is eaten with a spicy sauce (*wat*) of beans, vegetables, or meat. The *injera* serves as a utensil to scoop up this sauce. The highly versatile teff is also employed as the basis for brewing local alcoholic drinks known as *tela* and *katikala*. No part of the cereal goes to waste; teff straw is either fed to cattle or used for building wattle-and-daub walls.

Traders sifting teff at a market in Lalibela, Ethiopia. This widely used grain is the country's main staple cereal crop.

change under *gebbar*. Although Haile Selassie introduced more modern forms of taxation, the political power and privileges of the feudal lordships remained untouched. In particular, many wealthy Amhara were able to develop new agricultural areas to which they kept the land rights. These lands were then occupied by tenant farmers who remained subject to their masters. Centuries of Amhara domination caused resentment among Ethiopia's other peoples. The land reforms of the Derg revolutionary government after 1974 swept away the landlords, nationalized all farmland, and redistributed land to the common people. Although the extreme measures of the Derg eventually became hated, their land reforms initially won wide support and did much to redistribute wealth among the people of Ethiopia, Amhara and non-Amhara alike.

RELIGION AND CULTURE

Most Amhara belong to the Ethiopian Orthodox (Tewahido) Church, which has close links with the Coptic Church of Egypt. The Ethiopian Church's history spans some 1,600 years, and represents a unique and ancient form of Christianity. It holds sacred many religious texts that have been rejected by the Eastern Orthodox and Western (Roman Catholic and Protestant) Churches. The Ethiopian Bible is written in Ge'ez, an ancient Semitic language closely related to Amharic, and is organized differently to the familiar Christian Bible. In particular, the Tewahido Church's greater emphasis on Old Testament teachings makes it more similar

THE RASTAFARI MOVEMENT

The Rastafari movement is a religious movement that emerged among poor, working-class blacks in Jamaica in the early 20th century. It was based on the ideas of Marcus Garvey (1887–1940), founder of the Universal Negro Improvement Association, which promoted black self-empowerment and a "Return to Africa." Rastafarians believe that Ras Tafari (Crown Prince)—later Haile Selassie I, emperor of Ethiopia—was the Black Messiah, come to Earth to free his people. Their dedication to Ethiopia is reinforced by the notion (also held by Ethiopian Christians) that, because Ethiopians are thought to descend from the legendary Menelik I, son of Solomon and the Queen of Sheba, black people are the true Children of Israel, or Chosen People. Believing that their ancestors lost their African identity during slavery, Rastas aim to re-create their ties to nature by rejecting modern Western society, which they call Babylon; even their dreadlock hairstyle is an expression of their naturalness. Yet although Rastas see Ethiopia as their adopted nation (honoring the green, red, and gold colors of its flag and learning Amharic), very few Amhara have joined their movement.

to orthodox Judaism. Its other affinities to Judaism include dietary restrictions, such as not eating pork, separate areas of worship for men and women (as in conservative synagogues), and the requirement that women cover their hair with a head scarf (or *shash*) in church. Worshippers also remove their shoes when entering a church.

The foundation of the Ethiopian Church is associated with the sacred Jewish object known as the Ark of the Covenant, which contained the tablets of the Law that God gave to Moses. The Amhara believe that Menelik I made a copy of the Ark and

THE MURSI

The Mursi live in the remote Omo Valley in southwestern Ethiopia near the Sudanese border. Their homeland is surrounded by a mountain range and three rivers, isolating them from the rest of the country; when an anthropologist first visited the Mursi in the early 1970s, they had not even heard of Ethiopia. They have their own language and few are familiar with Amharic. With a population estimated at just 4,000, the Mursi live a nomadic cattle-herding life, with some crop growing. Sporadic cattle raids break out between them and neighboring peoples such as the Banna and the Bodi. Most Mursi follow their own traditional religion, though since the 1980s missionary activity in the region has succeeded in converting around 15 percent of the population to Christianity.

brought the real one to Axum. The Tewahido Church also has renowned artistic and architectural traditions, most notably the spectacular 13th-century churches at Lalibela cut from solid rock.

The Amhara speak Amharic, a Semitic language with its own distinctive script that was developed around 2,000 years ago.

SEE ALSO: *African-langage literature; Architecture; Christianity; Falasha; Festival and ceremony; Oromo.*

A young boy at the Rastafarian community of Shashemene in Ethiopia stands in front of a portrait of the movement's spiritual father, the former Amhara Emperor of Ethiopia, Haile Selassie.

Shop signs (right) in Amharic and English. The same script is used for the Amharic, Oromo, Tigrinya, and Tigre languages.

NOTABLE EAST AFRICAN BUILDINGS

City	Country	Building
Zanzibar	Tanzania	Old Dispensary
Lalibela	Ethiopia	Churches hewn from solid rock
Axum	Ethiopia	Stelae (pillars or obelisks)
Kampala	Uganda	Bugandan royal tombs
Kilwa Kisiwani	Tanzania	Great Mosque
Mombasa	Kenya	Fort Jesus

THE SCALE AND STYLE OF EAST AFRICAN ARCHITECTURE IS EXTREMELY VARIED. IT RANGES FROM TEMPORARY REED AND BRUSH SHELTERS CONSTRUCTED BY NOMADIC PEOPLES TO IMPOSING STONE TOWNS. ALONGSIDE AFRICAN BUILDING METHODS, MANY OUTSIDE INFLUENCES HAVE SHAPED THE BUILDINGS OF EAST AFRICA.

RURAL BUILDINGS

Traditional house-building methods are still used in many rural parts of East Africa. Walls are constructed from wattle (woven sticks), which are then covered with adobe (also called "daub") made from mud and dung. The daub dries and hardens in the sun. These dwellings are usually circular, measuring 6–18 feet (2–6 m) in diameter and 6–8 feet (2–2.5 m) in height with a single room and a conical thatched roof made of grass. The walls may be left bare or whitewashed and brightly painted, while the roof is often adorned with offerings or charms to ward off evil spirits. The most impressive buildings in this "beehive" style, which is common throughout sub-Saharan Africa, are the Bugandan royal tombs in Kampala, Uganda. The large central burial chamber there is 46 feet (14 m) in diameter and 39 feet (12 m) high.

In some regions, houses may be dug into the ground or mountainside, while stone is also sometimes used as a building material. More recently rectangular homes have become popular, along with materials such as corrugated iron and plastic sheeting. This

This settlement in Rwanda displays old and new building materials, with circular "beehive" houses surrounding a modern rectangular building with a tiled roof.

is especially the case in the shanty towns on the outskirts of many major cities.

Temporary structures made of reed, brush, or skins include the shelters built by the nomadic Somali and the igloo-shaped dwellings of the Elmolo people near Lake Turkana in Kenya.

HIGHLAND ETHIOPIA

Highland Ethiopia possesses some of the most impressive ancient architecture in Africa. The ruins of the kingdom that was based at Axum (first–seventh centuries C.E.) include ornate public buildings and magnificent cathedrals. Yet the most imposing Axumite monuments are tombs that are marked by large obelisks (stelae). Constructed between the third and fourth centuries, the six largest stelae range from 49 feet (15 m) to 108 feet (33 m) in height, while the largest, now collapsed, weighs 520 tons (472 tonnes). The stelae are made from solid granite and are covered with stylized carvings of architectural features such as lintels, doorways, windows, and inscriptions.

Also in Ethiopia are the extraordinary churches at Lalibela, once the country's capital. These 11 churches, which were built in the early 14th century and are still regularly used for worship, are cut entirely out of the solid rock of the hillside. The church of Bet Medhane Alem is the largest freestanding, rock-hewn building in the world.

COASTAL SWAHILI

Swahili architecture is a blend of African and Arabian styles, including pillared tombs, ornate coral stonework (notably on the island of Zanzibar), and ornate ceramic inlays. The oldest wooden mosque in East Africa (780 C.E.) was erected at Shanga near Lamu in Kenya. Many stone mosques were built later, including the Great Mosque (11th–13th centuries) at the trading center of Kilwa in southern Tanzania. This building incorporated pillars of solid coral and a large vaulted roof that is still standing today. The remains of Swahili "stone towns," with large private houses and grand palaces, are found along the Kenyan and Tanzanian coasts. These settlements are characterized by narrow, winding streets and elaborately carved doorways; ornate woodcarving, which reached its zenith in the 18th century, indicated a Swahili household's status. Later buildings of the colonial period are large and airy, with balustrades and balconies showing Arabic and Indian influences. The imposing Portuguese and Omani forts on the East African coast include Fort Jesus at Mombasa.

SEE ALSO: *Amhara; Christianity; Ganda; Islam; Somali; Swahili.*

Emperor Fasilidas of Ethiopia (r.1632–67) built this castle at the highland capital of Gondar to defend his Christian empire of Ethiopia from attacks by its Muslim neighbors.

CHRISTIANITY

TIMELINE

c.330	The Axumite kingdom converts to Christianity.
450	The Nine Saints, missionaries from Syria, arrive in Ethiopia and facilitate the spread of Christianity among the rural population.
1270	Ethiopia's "Solomonic" dynasty is established; the 11 rock-cut churches of Lalibela are built, and the *Kebra Nagast* (dynastic book of kings) is compiled.
1505	First Portuguese missionaries arrive in East Africa.
1698	Conquest of Mombasa by the Muslim Sultanate of Oman ends Portuguese plans to convert coastal peoples to Roman Catholicism.
1844	First Anglican missionaries in East Africa.
1880–90	Missionary activity expands in parallel with colonialism.
1930–40	Development of Kikuyu schools and religious sects.
1951	First Ethiopian Patriarch of the Ethiopian Orthodox Church is appointed, ending more than a thousand years of Egyptian-born (Coptic) appointees.
1975	Ethiopia's new Marxist government makes the country a republic and disengages the state from the Church.
1980s	Roman Catholic Church supports Hutu dominance in Rwanda and Burundi.
1993	Eritrean Orthodox Church gains independent status following Eritrea's independence from Ethiopia.

A prayer meeting in Rwanda. Christian groups are working to promote reconciliation between Hutu and Tutsi after the terrible genocide that swept this country and neighboring Burundi in 1994–95.

CHRISTIANITY IN EAST AFRICA HAS A VERY ANCIENT HISTORY, DATING TO THE FOUNDATION OF THE ETHIOPIAN ORTHODOX CHURCH IN THE FOURTH CENTURY. LATER MISSIONARIES, ESPECIALLY IN THE 19TH CENTURY, SPREAD THE FAITH TO KENYA, TANZANIA, UGANDA, RWANDA, AND BURUNDI.

THE ETHIOPIAN CHURCH

The Axumite kingdom in highland Ethiopia adopted Christianity in around 330 C.E. Legends trace the conversion to a Christian boy called Frumentius, who was shipwrecked on the Red Sea coast of Ethiopia and rose to prominence in the royal court. The church grew rapidly in the sixth century with the arrival of new missionaries from Syria and aligned itself with the Coptic Church of Egypt. Following the introduction of Islam to northeast Africa from the late seventh century onward, the Amharic speakers of the Ethiopian Highlands maintained their national identity through asserting their Christianity. The monasteries played a key role in this process. In the early 1600s the Portuguese tried but failed to impose Roman Catholicism on Ethiopia as the price for helping the Christian empire repel attacks by its Muslim neighbors. Throughout, Ethiopia remained true to its ancient faith. The church secured final independence from the Patriarchate of Alexandria in 1951, but was persecuted by the Marxist regime of Mengistu Haile Mariam that took power in 1974. Today about half the population of Ethiopia and Eritrea (which has had a separate church since independence) is Christian. An ancient Semitic language called Ge'ez is used in church services. Illuminated manuscripts and the astonishing rock-cut churches of Lalibela express Ethiopia's strong Christian artistic heritage.

The Church of St. George (Beta Ghiorghis) *is one of 11 churches at Lalibela in Ethiopia. Built in the late 13th century, they were cut out of the solid rock of the hillside; even the altars inside are an integral part of the original cliff face.*

EUROPEAN MISSIONARIES AND AFRICAN CHURCHES

The first European missions in East Africa were established by the Portuguese in 1505. However, they had little impact and largely disappeared when the Sultanate of Oman took control of the coast. Missionary activity began in earnest in 1844 when the German missionary Johan Ludwig Krapf landed at Mombasa and traveled inland. Others soon followed, including the explorer David Livingstone, whose chief aim was to wipe out the Arabian and Swahili slave trade in East Africa. By the 1880s missions had established themselves in Buganda and were having some success in concerting people. Missionary work went hand in hand with the European colonial takeover of Africa.

All of the main branches of Christianity were active in Africa at this time, including Methodism, Catholicism, and Scottish Presbyterianism. Often competing with each other, they brought African societies education and healthcare, and many people converted to take advantage of these benefits. The missions were particularly successful among freed slaves, the homeless, young people, and women. Many converts also found that they could win preferment in the colonial system.

Belief in a single, all-powerful God often accorded well with preexisting beliefs. Many people converted to the new faith, but combined it with traditional ritual practices. African sects emerged, for example among the Kikuyu, reflecting this blend of beliefs.

Many East African churches exist today. Although most remain aligned with their European mother churches, others preach a uniquely African form of Christianity.

The Church still plays a key role in people's lives, providing schools, orphanages, and welfare support. The Catholic Church was particularly influential in Rwanda and Burundi, but was criticized for the support that some of its clergy gave to those involved in the genocide of 1995–96.

SEE ALSO: African-language literature; Akan; Architecture; Festival and ceremony; Islam; Marriage and the family.

THE ARK OF THE COVENANT
The holiest site of the Ethiopian Orthodox Church is the church of Our Lady Mary of Zion at the ancient capital of Axum. The legendary first emperor of Ethiopia, Menelik I, son of King Solomon and the Queen of Sheba, is supposed to have brought to this place the Biblical Ark of the Covenant (the shrine made to hold the Ten Commandments that God gave to Moses). All Ethiopian churches have a *tabot*, a replica of the Ark, which is paraded at ceremonies, notably Timkat or Epiphany (a celebration of Christ's first manifestation of His divinity, which begins on January 6).

ARTISTS IN EAST AFRICA

Artist	Dates	Medium	Country
Henry Lumu	1862–1945	Painting	Uganda
Gregory Maloba	b.1922	Sculpture	Kenya
Sam Ntiro	1923–93	Painting	Tanzania
Elimo Njau	b.1932	Painting	Tanzania/Kenya
George Lilanga	b.1934	Painting/sculpture	Tanzania

MODERN ART IN EAST AFRICA IS CLOSELY ASSOCIATED WITH AN INNOVATIVE ART EDUCATION PROGRAM IN UGANDA IN THE 1930s. A UNIQUELY EAST AFRICAN STYLE DEVELOPED THAT IS STILL STRONGLY IN EVIDENCE IN CONTEMPORARY WORKS.

A local artist in Stone Town, on the Tanzanian island of Zanzibar, exhibits his paintings for sale. Many artists find a ready market for their work among the tourists who visit the island. East Africa has a thriving modern art scene, with painters and sculptors drawing on a wide range of influences in their work.

BEGINNINGS

The modern art scene in East Africa began with the opening of the Makerere School of Fine Arts in 1937. Founded and run by an English art historian, Margaret Trowell, the school trained several generations of budding young artists. Many of them went on to become leading figures in the African arts scene. The Makerere School was the only higher education institute in the entire region at that time. It provided an intellectually stimulating forum for students from all over East Africa to explore their creative potential. The end result was the development of a uniquely East African style. In common with many people at that time, Trowell believed that Africans thought in a different way to Westerners, and consequently thought that any exposure to European art would be a corrupting influence on the students. Accordingly, she banned all prints of Western art and art books from the school, and instead encouraged her students to develop their artistic imagination through the use of traditional storytelling, in particular religious stories. From a modern perspective, the thinking behind Trowell's method may seem misguided and based on racial stereotypes, but the results were spectacular. Painters such as the Tanzanians Sam Ntiro and Elimo Njau, and sculptors such as the Kenyans Gregory Maloba and Rosemary Namuli produced unique, important works.

THE "UGANDA SCHOOL"

In 1958 Trowell retired, and the Art School was taken over by the South African Cecil Todd. Todd ended the earlier teaching methods and began to introduce students to European art history. As a result, during the 1960s, the output began to show signs of Western influence. Yet through the work of students such as Ugandan painters David Kibuuka, David Kitamirike, and Henry Lumu, it also continued to develop a uniquely East African style. These artists are often referred to as the "Uganda School." A major source of inspiration for them was Cubism (the painting of Picasso and Braque in the early 20th century), with its emphasis on fragmentation and geometric forms. This influence was blended with vibrant colors and East African themes—such as local cultural practices and landscapes.

Students at the second modern art school to open in East Africa, the Ethiopian School of Fine Arts and Design (founded 1957),

produced a very similar type of synthesis. This particular style has continued to define modern art across East Africa. In the 1970s and 1980s, political instability forced most Ugandan artists to leave East Africa. Today, more are based in California and New York than in Kampala or Nairobi. However, new generations of artists—many of them students of former Makerere graduates—are sustaining a thriving East African art scene.

Paintings and sculptures by the Tanzanian artist George Lilanga. His work often shows cartoonlike figures, and draws on the sculptural traditions of his own Makonde people. Lilanga has gained an international reputation.

SEE ALSO: *Festival and ceremony; Sculpture; Textiles.*

THE PAA-YA-PAA CENTER, NAIROBI

In 1965, a number of former students of the Makerere School—led by Elimo Njau—opened the Paa-ya-Paa ("the antelope rises") Art Center outside Nairobi, Kenya. Originally set up to showcase East African sculpture, it soon began to promote East African painting as well. During the 1970s, several members of the Uganda School exhibited there, and used it to train a second generation of modern artists. Paa-ya-Paa still plays a key role on the East African art scene, especially since the foundation of a UNESCO-funded artist-in-residence scheme in the 1980s.

DANCE AND SONG

DANCE COMPANIES

Company	City/Country
Compagnie Gaara	Nairobi, Kenya
Footsteps Dance Company	Kampala, Uganda
Ndere Troupe	Kampala, Uganda
Adugna Community Dance Theater	Addis Ababa, Ethiopia
Mionzi Dance Theater	Dar-es-Salaam, Tanzania

DANCE AND SONG IN EAST AFRICA ARE NOT JUST PERFORMED BY SPECIALISTS FOR AN AUDIENCE. RATHER, WHOLE COMMUNITIES PARTICIPATE IN THE DANCES, WHOSE FORMS COME FROM THE EXPERIENCES OF DAILY LIFE.

THE ROLE OF DANCE AND SONG.

Song and dance, which form an integral part of most societies, perform a variety of social roles. Singing and dancing can be used to relieve physical or mental tension, or may be performed as part of a competition. They can be used to display a person's physical prowess; alternatively, they may tell a story or give praise. Lyrics and body movements may be used to reinforce or to challenge social norms. Finally, among peoples who lack a written history, they fulfil the important function of preserving folk memory.

Among African peoples, all of the diverse purposes that singing and dancing serve are intimately connected with the daily life of a community. Song and dance are far from being just superficial entertainment. They help break down social barriers, encourage the formation of relationships, and are often performed at ceremonies marking the key rites of passage of birth, initiation into adulthood, marriage, and death.

Ngoma dancers in Tanzania perform with nuts tied around their ankles as instruments. Ngoma means "drum and dance" in Swahili and expresses the close connection between music and dance in East African societies.

THE SAUTI ZA BUSARA SWAHILI MUSIC FESTIVAL

The Sauti za Busara ("Sounds of Wisdom") Swahili Music Festival on the Tanzanian island of Zanzibar was established in 2003. In 2005 the four-day festival played host to more than 40 groups and 450 artists, many of whom had traveled from places as far away as Uganda, Egypt, Yemen, Zimbabwe, and Rwanda. The variety of styles included Sufi Muslim groups, drum and dance (*ngoma*) groups, Gogo music and dance from the Dodoma region of central Tanzania, guitar bands, and traditional Swahili *taarab* singing. Hip-hop sensations from around the region also attended in force, including popular acts such as Juma Nature and Wanaume Family from Tanzania, Klear Kut from Uganda, and Wazenji Kijiwe from Zanzibar. Among the festival favorites were the women's Imena Dance Group from Rwanda and the Tanzanian queen of East African popular music, Saida Karoli.

DANCES OF WAR AND OF LOVE

Song and dance in East Africa are often performed in the context of traditional rites peculiar to particular peoples. For example, in the past the Kamba people, who live in the Ukambana Hills of central Kenya, were renowned for their acrobatic dances. To the accompaniment of "Akamba" drums playing in different, complex rhythms, male dancers would perform spectacular leaps, flip-flops, and somersaults. The Kamba dance tradition has now largely died out, however.

Dance rituals that are still thriving and widely known include the "warrior" dances of the Maasai and Samburu. These dances, which are performed by young men recently initiated into adulthood, direct ritualized aggression not just at external enemies, but also at senior age-groups in the community whose status the dancers aim to challenge. Such dances may also be used to attract partners and courtship dances are common. Often dance ceremonies are an opportunity for the normal rules of etiquette and reserve to be set aside and for "mock" advances and challenges to be made. Among the Geleb of southwest Ethiopia, for example, courtship

dances can be very playful and provocative. Men indicate their choice of dance partner by thrusting their hips and the dance ends with the couples closely entwined.

Lyrical competitions are also widespread, at which individuals win acclaim for their skillful use of language. Popular subjects include lovers and cattle, although songs of praise directed toward deities or spirits are also common. Christians and Muslims sing particular religious songs both as an act of worship and as an expression of their religious identity.

Kikuyu dancers in Kenya prepare for a performance of a dance associated with the initiation rite.

BETA ISRAEL DANCE AND SONG

Ethiopia's Jews, the Beta Israel, traditionally performed a "shoulder" dance similar to that of their mainly Christian Amhara neighbors. In this style, dancers put their hands on their hips and move only their shoulders and heads. Some dancers move both shoulders at the same time, either vertically or horizontally, while others thrust each shoulder individually. Dance troupes that have grown up among the Ethiopian Jews who resettled in Israel have radically reinterpreted this style. The Esketa Dance group, for example, have fused traditional Beta Israel and other Ethiopian folk dances with modern artistic and dance-club steps. They also incorporate prayers and songs into their performances. Esketa have performed widely in France and North America, winning critical acclaim.

During the colonial era certain styles of dance and song were formalized and came to be regarded as markers of ethnic identity. Such dances were often performed at major public functions, or at hotels for the benefit of tourists. These formal styles are still taught in schools today and performed at national dance competitions. Yet from these rather stereotyped dance forms arose new forms of music, such as Benga and Lingala (see MUSIC AND MUSICAL INSTRUMENTS).

MODERN STYLES

Modern East African music and dance are rediscovering their roots and going beyond the standardized forms of the colonial period. Many dance groups now draw on modern and disco-dance moves from the West or Asia. The new fusion styles that they have created can be seen in bars, clubs, and theaters throughout the region. Rap music has become extremely popular, with each country developing its own unique style. Stars of hip-hop regularly play to audiences of thousands. Today East Africa is a hotbed of innovative modern music and dance, yet they have not yet made the breakthrough into the Western market that has occurred more notably with the music of West Africa.

SEE ALSO: Falasha; Festival and ceremony; Kikuyu; Maasai; Music and musical instruments; Oral literature; Swahili.

MAASAI EUNOTO DANCES

The three-day Maasai Eunoto ceremony, at which an entire age-grade of Maasai young men moves from youth to adulthood, is marked by much dancing and singing. Dressed as warriors, youths gather on the first day to perform the Red Dance, which symbolizes their ferocity and bravery. Praises are sung to those who have distinguished themselves by killing a lion. The most famous part of the dance is the *empatia* (right), in which the warriors leap high into the air, moving their shoulders in time to their rhythmic chanting. On landing the youths flick their long, ochered hair toward their partners standing nearby. These watching girls also dance rhythmically and shake their beaded jewelry in time with the dancing.

FACT FILE

Population	Estimated at 350,000, including Tanzania (250,000), Kenya (70,000), and Uganda (10,000)
Religion	Hinduism, Islam, Christianity, Sikhism, Zoroastrianism
Language	Hindi, Gujarati, Kachchi, Panjabi. Many East African Asians also use English as a business language.

TIMELINE

1st century c.e. on	Traders from the Arabian Peninsula and western India trade with East Africa.
c.1000–1500	Islam introduced to East African coastal region, as far south as present-day Tanzania.
1832	Sultanate of Zanzibar established as Sultan of Oman moves his capital from Muscat in Arabia.
1885–1900	Britain and Germany partition East Africa into colonies.
1895–1901	Britain imports Indian indentured laborers to build the Uganda Railroad (the so-called "Lunatic Line").
1914	East African Indian National Congress formed.
1961–63	Tanganyika (now Tanzania), Uganda, Kenya, and Zanzibar win their independence.
1966–79	Democracy ends in Uganda with the rule of the dictators Milton Obote and Idi Amin.
1972	Asians summarily expelled from Uganda by Amin; they settle in Britain, Canada, Australia, and New Zealand.
1982	Anti-Asian rioting in Kenya follows failed military coup.
1992	Ugandan president Yoweri Museveni invites Asians to return.
2005	Kenyan voters reject a proposed new constitution.

PERMANENT SETTLERS FROM ASIA MIGRATED TO EAST AFRICA IN TWO DISTINCT WAVES IN THE 19TH CENTURY. DURING THE COLONIAL ERA AND AFTER INDEPENDENCE, EAST AFRICAN ASIANS MADE VITAL CONTRIBUTIONS TO GOVERNMENT, INDUSTRY, AND COMMERCE.

EARLY CONTACTS

Traders and travelers from Asia have been moving up and down the East African coast since at least the first century C.E. Merchants in dhows (cargo-carrying sailboats) used the winds of the "winter" monsoon, from November to February, to cross from Western India and Arabia and trade in cotton, ivory, pottery, spices, and slaves. They would return with the "summer" monsoon (April–October). Even today, thousands of migrant traders still ply their trade across the Indian Ocean.

From the early 19th century onward, increasing numbers of Asians began to settle permanently on the coast. Migration increased after the Sultan of Oman, Said ibn

East African Asian families arrive in Britain after being thrown out of Uganda.

THE UGANDAN EXPULSIONS

In 1972, the Ugandan dictator Idi Amin suddenly ordered all the country's 80,000 Asians holding a British passport to leave within 90 days. The expulsions were part of his deliberate policy of Africanizing Uganda's trade and industry. In this move, the Asians lost everything they had built up over many decades, being required to surrender all their property. Amin's dramatic gesture misfired badly; without the Asians' extensive credit networks and their industrial and business know-how, the country's economy soon collapsed. Uganda's loss was other countries' gain. The Asians' skills and enterprise greatly benefited Britain, and especially the city of Leicester where many refugees settled. In 1992, President Yoweri Museveni invited the Ugandan Asians back; since then Asians have reclaimed 98 percent of their former property.

Worshippers celebrate the founding of a new Sikh temple (gurdwara) in Kenya. Sikhs, originally from India's Punjab region, are just one of the Asian groups that have enriched East African life.

Sultan (1791–1856) relocated his capital from Arabia to the island of Zanzibar in 1832. Said immediately appointed a number of Muslim Indians to senior positions in the Sultanate of Zanzibar. When the British duly signed a trade pact with the Sultanate in 1847 all British subjects—including Indians—were guaranteed the right to enter Zanzibar, and to live and trade there. In the following decades, several thousand more Indian traders—mostly Hindus from Gujarat in northwest India—set up permanent residence in the Sultan's domain, which also embraced the coast of present-day Tanzania.

THE SECOND WAVE

A second wave of Asian migrants arrived in East Africa at the end of the 19th century, drafted in as indentured (contracted) laborers by the British to build the Uganda Railroad. Begun in 1895, this railroad ran from Mombasa on the Kenyan coast to Kisumu on Lake Victoria (it was later extended to the Ugandan capital Kampala). Around 15,000 Indian laborers worked on the railroad, mostly Christians from Goa

(a Portuguese-controlled territory on India's west coast). When the railroad was completed in 1902, many Goans decided to stay on in Kenya, notably in Mombasa and Nairobi. Because they were barred both from the professions and from owning land, they created their own employment in small-scale trading and market gardening. Yet their generally high level of education—many families sent their children back to school in India—also helped them secure jobs in the colonial civil service.

THE 20TH CENTURY

By around 1910, many Muslim Indians from the coast had risen to high office in the colonial administration. Others were emerging as leading businessmen (in manufacturing, mining, textiles, tourism, and other sectors). Gujarati traders worked in every urban or commercial center in East Africa. Thanks to their extended trade and credit networks, which often stretched back to India itself, they came to control almost all the region's trade. Goans were prominent in the civil service, particularly as tax and buildings inspectors and as teachers. All the Indian communities developed extensive social and cultural networks, in the form of sports clubs, charitable foundations, and so on. Yet because these institutions mostly excluded black Africans, they also helped sow the seeds of resentment and suspicion.

Today, in Kenya, Rwanda, Uganda, Tanzania, and elsewhere, Indians often still play key roles in government, industry, trade, and education. Yet the separateness that had characterized their communities under colonialism occasionally led to conflict in post-independence East Africa. The most notorious episode was when Idi Amin expelled all Asians from Uganda in 1972 (see box feature).

SEE ALSO: Architecture; English-language literature; Ganda; Kikuyu; Maasai; Nyoro; Swahili.

MAJOR WORKS AND THEIR AUTHORS

Title	Date	Author	Country
Uganda's Katikiro in London	1904	Ham Mukasa	Uganda
Out of Africa	1937	Karen Blixen	Kenya
Facing Mount Kenya	1938	Jomo Kenyatta	Kenya
The Flame Trees of Thika	1959	Elspeth Huxley	Kenya
Weep Not, Child The River Between	1964 1965	Ngugi wa Thiong'o (then called James Ngugi)	Kenya
The Promised Land	1966	Grace Ogot	Uganda
Song of Lawino Song of Ocol	1966 1970	Okot p'Bitek	Uganda
Child of Two Worlds	1967	Mugo Gatheru	Kenya
Dying in the Sun	1967	Peter Palangyo	Tanzania
Faces at the Crossroads: A "Currents" Anthology	1971	Chris Wanjala (ed.)	Uganda
In a Brown Mantle The General is Up	1972 1991	Peter Nazareth	Uganda
Groping in the Dark	1974	Barnabas Katigula	Tanzania
Abyssinian Chronicles Snakepit	2001 2005	Moses Isegawa	Uganda

ENGLISH-LANGUAGE LITERATURE DEVELOPED QUITE LATE IN EAST AFRICA. YET AS THE 20TH CENTURY PROGRESSED, LOCAL WRITERS USED ENGLISH TO VOICE CRITICISM OF COLONIAL AND POSTINDEPENDENCE GOVERNMENTS. BUT POLITICAL REPRESSION HAS TAKEN ITS TOLL, DRIVING MANY EAST AFRICAN WRITERS INTO EXILE ABROAD.

HISTORY

English language literature only emerged relatively late in East Africa, long after it had been established in the western and southern parts of the continent. Even by the mid-1960s, very little had been published by East African writers in English, except for a few personal memoirs and history books. Certainly, there were no English-language literary figures of the stature of, say, Nigeria's Amos Tutuola and Wole Soyinka.

There are a number of explanations for this late start. The primary reason was that East Africa had a much longer heritage of local language literatures than other parts of the continent. So, even after the arrival of Europeans, most East African authors continued to produce works in their own languages, and saw no reason to adopt written English. In addition, early forms of Western education in East Africa were provided first by missionary societies and later by colonial administrations; they stressed the importance of literacy skills in local languages and gave little attention to literary English. The type of education on offer in the early decades of the 20th century

The Danish-born writer Karen Blixen (1885–1962) lived for many years in Kenya, where she wrote the novel Out of Africa *(later a major Hollywood film). This book, describing her farm and her love of East Africa, was written under the name of Isak Dinesen.*

university graduates produced a steady stream of writings. These were mostly autobiographies and studies of African peoples. The most famous work of this time was Jomo Kenyatta's study of his native ethnic group, the Kikuyu, *Facing Mount Kenya* (1938). Kenyatta published this book when he was still a student at the London School of Economics. Also during the 1930s and 1940s, a number of white Kenyan settlers produced works that were based directly on, or inspired by, their experiences. These writers included Elspeth Huxley (1907–97) and Karen Blixen. Yet by the early 1960s, there was still no distinct English-language fiction, poetry, or drama.

(Far left) Jomo Kenyatta (1892–1978), Kenya's first president after independence, pictured with his family in the early 20th century. The study he wrote of the Kikuyu (Facing Mount Kenya) *showed his people's way of life already under threat from Western influence.*

A DISTINCT VOICE

The key event in the development of a distinctly East African literature in English was the African Writers Conference of 1962. Held in Kampala, Uganda, this forum brought together writers, critics, and publishers from throughout English-speaking Africa and the Diaspora (Africans who had emigrated abroad). Yet despite taking place in East Africa, the conference attracted very few contributions from the region. Rather, the quality of work from West and Southern

also emphasized vocational (that is, practical career) skills rather than academic skills. Since colonial occupation came later to East Africa than to other parts of the continent, the chief concern of the first European governors was to build up their new administrations fast. Accordingly, their need was for bureaucrats, not creative writers. Finally, because English had arrived late it had not yet had a chance to develop its own distinctive "local voice," which became such an important factor in the writings of West African English-language authors.

FIRST STEPS

It was not until the first East Africans began to travel to Europe for college education, from about 1920 on, that English-language publishing began in earnest. Before that time, only a very few works had been produced, such as the account written by the prime minister of the Kingdom of Buganda, Ham Mukasa (1870–1956), of his trip to London in 1902 (*Uganda's Katikiro in London*; 1904). With the encouragement of their Western teachers, the new generation of

NGUGI WA THIONG'O

Ngugi wa Thiong'o (b.1938) is Kenya's most famous novelist. As James Ngugi, he achieved worldwide acclaim with two novels, *Weep Not, Child* (1964) and *The River Between* (1965). Both novels criticized European colonialism, although in a different way to the work of, say, the Ugandan writer Okot p'Bitek. Rather than looking at colonialism's broad impact on society, Ngugi's novels examined colonialism and the violence it bred from the point of view of the individual. *Weep Not* tells of a young man's failed attempts to receive a higher education, while *The River* recounts an individual's quest to find love during the time of the Mau Mau rebellion. Increasingly influenced by Marxist ideas, during the 1970s Ngugi changed his name and announced that he would no longer publish in English but would write in his native Gikuyu and in Swahili (see African-language literature). In 1977 Ngugi was jailed for a political satire in Gikuyu. This repression eventually persuaded him, in 1982, to exile himself to London.

OKOT P'BITEK

One of the most important members of the Makerere writers' circle in Uganda in the 1960s was the poet Okot p'Bitek (1931–82). An ethnic Acholi by birth, p'Bitek at first wrote several books in his native Luo language. He then published what was to become his most influential work in English, *Song of Lawino* (1966). Four years later, he produced a sequel, *Song of Ocol*. These two works, which are written in the style of Acholi songs, examine the impact of European colonialism on African society. The poems narrate the trials and tribulations of a husband and wife. The husband (Lawino) symbolizes the forces of modernity and change, while the wife (Ocol) represents traditional roles and responsibilities.

Africa, in particular, showed local writers what was possible. At the same time the lack of East African literature was a cause of embarrassment, and acted as a spur to delegates to remedy the situation. The 1962 conference turned out to be an important stimulus, and over the next decade the output of East African writers increased dramatically.

At the forefront of this development were writers attached to the English Department of Makerere University College in Kampala, Uganda—an institution set up in 1939 to provide higher education for all of British East Africa. They produced what were to become some of the classics of East African literature. The Ugandan poet Okot p'Bitek and Kenyan essayist and novelist Ngugi wa Thiong'o studied there. Other important writers to emerge from Makerere were the Ugandan Asian essayist Peter Nazareth (b.1940), Tanzanian novelist Barnabas Katigula (b.1935), and Ugandan feminist writer Grace Ogot (b.1930). A common theme for all these writers was their powerful criticism of colonialism. They examined the relationship between tradition and modernity, and the challenges posed to African society by the arrival of European culture. The output of regional writers was so great during the 1960s that by 1971 the East African Writers Conference (in Nairobi) was able to showcase only work being produced by East African writers. It was a measure the optimism of the time that the main theme of the conference was future directions for East African literature. Yet this new-found optimism proved to be shortlived.

DECLINE AND REPRESSION

By the late 1970s, a number of factors had conspired to once again reduce the output of East African writers to barely a trickle. To date, it has not managed to recover from this position.

One major problem was the withdrawal by international publishers from the region, and the collapse of local publishing houses at the same time. In the 1960s, several international publishers established a presence in East Africa. At the same time, various local enterprises began to publish English-language books. These publishers included the East African Literature Bureau, originally set up by the British to bring out only African-language works. This growth of publishing opportunities helped stimulate the prolific output of writers at this time. However, by the 1970s, local markets for literature had begun to dry up. Economic hardship meant that fewer and fewer people could afford to buy books. And for those

At Kakimakoi in Kenya, a teacher at an outdoor class teaches literacy skills to adult learners.

THE MEMORY PROJECT

One of the most moving examples of East African writing in recent times has arisen from a continent-wide tragedy. In 1998, in a response to the HIV/AIDS epidemic, a group called NACWOLA (National Community of Women Living with HIV/AIDS) in Uganda set up the Memory Project. This program encourages infected parents and their children to make "memory books" together, scrapbooks containing shared experiences and thoughts. This activity helps them cope in some way with the impact of the disease. The books also help them through the healing process after the death of their parents and become their most treasured possession. More than 40,000 women now belong to NACWOLA, and the Memory Project is being extended to other African countries.

who could still afford it, international literature proved far more popular than locally produced works.

This situation was partly a reflection of the subject matter of East African literature. Criticism of colonialism had been a fresh topic in the 1960s but looked tired and dated by the 1970s. By then, all thoughts of colonial legacies had been replaced by concern with new political realities. Uganda was under the brutal, chaotic regime of Idi Amin, while Kenya was entering a period of severe economic decline. Local readers

As part of the Memory Project, the U.S. writer Joyce Maynard talks to a group of children in Uganda in 2000.

apparently felt that international English writers addressed these issues better than the home-grown authors.

These new political climate also stifled output. Throughout East Africa, post-independence governments were mostly suspicious of writers and their ability to stir up discontent. Over time, one author after another was either imprisoned or went into exile. Even by the late 1960s, most of the Makerere group had left Uganda, mainly for Europe and America. By the mid-1970s, the creative wave had ended. Since then, local writing collectives have produced a limited number of works, and some important writers have emerged from the East African Diaspora (for example Moses Isegawa). But these have been the exception rather than the rule. Most writers who left in the 1970s were not taken up by Western publishers. With hindsight, the 1960s now appear as the "golden age" of East African English-language writing.

MOSES ISEGAWA

The Ugandan Moses Isegawa is one of a new generation of East African authors writing in English. Born in 1963, Isegawa worked as a history teacher before leaving for the Netherlands in 1990. His first novel, *Abyssinian Chronicles* (2001), develops the tradition of writers like Ngugi. Recounting the story of a young boy growing up during the murderous regime of Idi Amin (1971–79), it deals with the relationship between the individual and a society marred by violence. It can also be read as a criticism of the colonial legacy that allowed people like Amin to come to power. Isegawa's second novel, *Snakepit* (2005), explores the corruption and lack of vision of the postcolonial Ugandan state.

SEE ALSO: *African-language literature; Contemporary art; Kikuyu; Oral literature.*

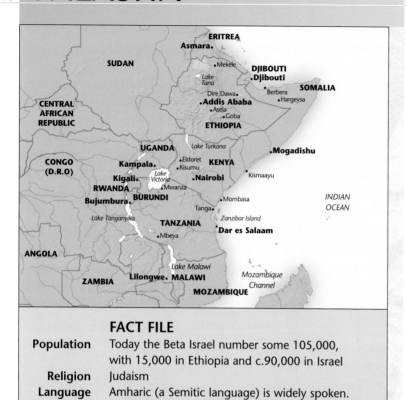

FACT FILE

Population	Today the Beta Israel number some 105,000, with 15,000 in Ethiopia and c.90,000 in Israel
Religion	Judaism
Language	Amharic (a Semitic language) is widely spoken. Ge'ez is solely a religious language; Falasha in Israel speak Hebrew.

TIMELINE

966–922 B.C.E.	Reign of King Solomon of Israel.
330	Introduction of Christianity to highland Ethiopia.
c.800–900	The stories of Eldad ha-Dani, which explain Falasha descent from the tribe of Dan, are written.
1860	First contact with the wider Jewish community.
1974	Ethiopian socialist regime (Derg) of Colonel Mengistu persecutes the Beta Israel.
1975	Israel officially recognizes the Beta Israel as descendants of the "Ten Lost Tribes" of Israel.
1980	Operations begin to bring Ethiopian Jews to Israel.
1984	Massive famine and conflict in Ethiopia lead to migrations of Ethiopian Jews into the Sudan. Operation Moses flies them from Sudan to Israel.
1985	Pressure from Arab nations ends Operation Moses, but a secret mission brings Jews left in Sudan to Israel.
1991	"Operation Solomon" transports thousands of Ethiopian Jews from Sudan and Ethiopia to Israel.
1996	Ethiopian Jews protest in Israel against discrimination.
2004	Israel proposes taking in all the remaining 15,000 Jews in Ethiopia.

THE FALASHA OR BETA ISRAEL ("HOUSE OF ISRAEL") ARE AN ETHIOPIAN JEWISH GROUP WITH UNKNOWN ORIGINS. THEY WERE ONLY OFFICIALLY RECOGNIZED AS JEWS IN 1975 BY THE AUTHORITIES IN ISRAEL, WHERE MANY OF THEM HAVE SINCE RESETTLED.

HISTORY

Many theories surround the origins of the Falasha (a term meaning "invaders" given to them by the Ethiopian neighbors). A 1,000-year-old text known as the *Kebra Nagast* ("Book of the Glory of the Kings of Ethiopia") claims that the father of the Ethiopian people, Menelik I, was the son of King Solomon of Israel and Bilqis, the Queen of Sheba. A different account traces their origins to the Jewish tribe of Dan, who tried to avoid civil war in the Kingdom of

Israel by resettling in Egypt. From there they moved south up the Nile into Ethiopia. Other sources suggest that the Beta Israel descend from Jews whom Ptolemy I (322–285 B.C.E.) brought to Egypt as prisoners of war, and who later settled in Nubia. Recent genetic studies indicate that the the Falasha are most closely related to their non-Jewish Ethiopian neighbors, making it more likely that their forbears were in fact Ethiopian Jewish converts rather than migrants.

Whatever their origin, the Falasha were isolated from mainstream Jewish culture for many centuries. This has made their integration into Israeli society very difficult.

SOCIETY AND DAILY LIFE

In rural Ethiopia the Beta Israel live in small adobe homes similar to those of surrounding peoples. Most are farmers, although a small proportion earn a living making crafts from metals, ceramics, and textiles. However, their religion and culture set them apart from

RESETTLEMENT IN ISRAEL

The oppressive Marxist regime in Ethiopia (1974–91) persecuted the Beta Israel, forcing them to resettle away from their heartland north of Lake Tana. By 1980 the Israelis had begun smuggling Ethiopian Jews out of the country. When a terrible famine hit Ethiopia in 1984, some 8,000 Jewish refugees who had fled to Sudan were airlifted out in the massive Operation Moses. A second secret mission (Operation Joshua), organized by the CIA, later rescued around 1,000 Jews left behind when Sudan halted the exodus. Further migration was banned by Ethiopia until the regime changed in 1991. With the country in turmoil, more than 14,000 Falasha were covertly flown to Israel in Operation Solomon. Since the first migrations, more than 80 percent of the Beta Israel—some 90,000 people—have resettled in Israel under that country's Law of Return.

Ethiopian Jewish children bound for Israel in 1991. Community support and religious education have helped the Falasha in the difficult process of integrating into their new homeland.

their Christian and Muslim neighbors, and they generally live in separate villages or in separate quarters in cities.

The Beta Israel in Ethiopia do not have the rabbis (teachers and religious leaders) found elsewhere in Judaism. Instead, religious authorities known as *kessim* lead the community, advising on spiritual, ceremonial, and legal matters. Community elders are also widely respected.

RELIGION AND CULTURE

The Beta Israel follow a modified form of Judaism that has been mostly bypassed by the post-Biblical developments in mainstream Judaism. The most holy book is the Torah, and a number of other texts are also revered, but the Talmud (interpretations of Jewish law) was unknown. The ancient Ethiopian Semitic dialect of Ge'ez is used in religious services, rather than Hebrew. Falasha retain animal sacrifice, Sabbath regulations, and dietary prohibitions, while the center of religious life is the *masjid*, or synagogue. In the past, villages were built near water sources to facilitate the cleansing rituals that surround menstruation, birth, death, and preparation for the Sabbath.

SEE ALSO: African-language literature; Afar; Amhara; Christianity; Dance and song; Islam; Metalwork.

MAJOR EVENTS IN EAST AFRICA

Maasai Eunoto (Kenya & Tanzania)	Transition of Maasai men into elderhood. Hundreds of Maasai from Kenya and Tanzania gather to sing, dance, and relinquish their prized warrior status.	Every 7–8 years
Karamajong Asapan (NW Uganda)	Pubescent Karamojong boys gather to ceremonially slaughter an ox, which is then ritually eaten. The ceremony marks their transition into adulthood.	Approximately every 7–8 years
Omo cattle and courtship dances (SW Ethiopia)	Omo men dance in imitation of their cattle, raising their hands in the air in the shape of horns to attract women.	Throughout the year, based on various seasonal occasions
Timkat (Ethiopia)	Christian celebration of Epiphany during which the *tabots* (replicas of the Ark of the Covenant) are paraded through towns.	January
Ramadan (Islamic areas)	Islamic month of fasting culminating in major celebrations, involving music, dancing, and feasting	Varies according to lunar calendar
Mombasa Carnival (Kenya)	Carnival displaying flamboyant floats and costumes from around Africa and the world.	November

E**AST AFRICA POSSESSES A RICH VARIETY OF COLORFUL CULTURAL EVENTS. THESE EVENTS RANGE FROM LONG-PRACTICED CEREMONIES SUCH AS INITIATION RITES, RAINMAKING CEREMONIES, AND DIVINATION, TO MODERN MUSIC FESTIVALS, CARNIVALS, AND ARTS CONVENTIONS.**

FESTIVAL AND CEREMONY

It is difficult to classify or categorize the huge range of cultural events that take place each year in East Africa. However, a basic distinction can be made between festivals that commemorate or celebrate an occasion and ritualistic ceremonies that have some physical, symbolic, or supernatural purpose. Yet there are no hard and fast rules and many events will be both festival and ceremony at the same time.

Ceremonies are incredibly diverse in form. They include events associated with major world religions such as Christianity (including the Ethiopian Orthodox Church),

Islam, and Judaism, various life-cycle ceremonies that bring about a change in a person's status, ceremonies designed to please deities or spirits (often involving some form of sacrifice), and rituals that aim to cause harm, heal, or protect. The variety is endless, and many events comprise a mixture of these elements. Also, new ceremonial forms that mix traditional and modern elements are constantly being devised. This is particularly true in relation to the spread of world religions such as Christianity and Islam.

RELIGIOUS FESTIVALS AND CEREMONIES

Christian highland Ethiopia has a great variety of festivals and ceremonies. These include Meskal, a two day festival celebrating the Finding of the True Cross, Fasika (Easter), Enkutatash (New Year), Ledet (Christmas), and Timkat (Epiphany). Muslims throughout the region celebrate typical Islamic observances and festivals, such as Eid ul-Fitr, Eid ul-Adha, Mawlid an-Nabi (the birthday of the prophet Muhammad) and Muharram (New Year).

ETHIOPIAN TIMKAT

This colorful three-day festival is the Ethiopian Orthodox Church's celebration of Epiphany. It is marked by the procession of *tabots*, replicas of the Ark of the Covenant, which are removed from churches and paraded around towns, draped in elaborately embroidered textiles. The processions are accompanied by singing, drumming, ringing of bells, and blowing of trumpets. People bathe in lakes and rivers and splash water on onlookers. The festivities continue throughout the night. The following day church services are held in honor of the archangel Michael and further festivities follow.

In the past various ceremonies were held in honor of traditional deities and spirits, but today these have largely been eroded by the spread of Christianity and Islam. In preexisting religions, prayers and requests were directed at deities and spirits on a regular basis. However, at important times of crisis (such as drought, disease, or war) more formal communal ceremonies were performed. Common means of appeasing or communicating with supernatural forces often included gifts of agricultural produce, beer, or sacrificial animals. The Kikuyu still hold a rainmaking ceremony that involves killing a lamb (see box feature). Gods and spirits were also often called upon to heal the sick or safeguard the metalworkers'

White-robed monks of the Ethiopian Orthodox Church gather at Lalibela in highland Ethiopia to celebrate the feast of Timkat. They blow trumpets, while at the foot of the cliff they are standing on, priests dance and sing.

KIKUYU RAINMAKING

If rain fails to fall in Kikuyuland in Kenya the elders will gather and summon the diviners, or seers, who inform them how Ngai (the Kikuyu God) may be appeased. The seers describe a specific animal—often a lamb with a unique color pattern—that can be used in sacrifice to Ngai. The elders search around the community for such an animal. On finding an appropriate lamb, suitable, "pure" participants (often the very young or the very old) and an ideal location for the ceremony are chosen. Then the day is set on which the ceremony will take place. Ritual prohibitions surround those involved and last some eight days. On the morning of the sacrifice a procession of the elders approaches the sacred tree under which the ceremony will occur. Prayers are chanted and the procession circles the tree before the animal is strangled and eaten. A portion of the meat is reserved as an offering to Ngai.

Kikuyu dancers at the traditional rainmaking ceremony that is held in honor of the supreme god Ngai.

craft or the harvest. Seasonal ceremonies accompanied the agricultural cycle.

Most societies included a variety of ceremonial specialists who ranged from castes of priests dedicated to maintaining the shrines of deities to prophets or seers. The seers were born with the special skill of being able to communicate with the supernatural world. This sometimes involved calling up spirits and acting as oracles for the community by foretelling events. Medicine men or women were also common, who drew their powers from their mastery in the use of medicinal or ritual substances. Some of these substances have effects that have since been confirmed by modern medical science, while others worked on a purely supernatural level. Divination ceremonies, which were designed to find out the root causes of misfortunes that had befallen the community, were also common.

LIFE-CYCLE CEREMONIES

Throughout Africa the human life-cycle is celebrated in ceremonies that mark the transition between the various stages in a person's life. Such ceremonies include rites associated with birth, puberty, initiation into adulthood and elderhood, marriage, the gaining of positions of responsibility in a community, and death.

Life-cycle ceremonies do not just symbolize or celebrate the transitions. They are often actually designed to create the capacities and attributes associated with the individual's new status. Thus, they incorporate periods of learning and trial that test the individual's ability to fulfil his or her new role. What is more, the people who are in a state of transition may be vulnerable to attack by evil forces, or may themselves be regarded as polluting or dangerous to the community. Life-cycle ceremonies therefore also have the purpose of protecting the individual and/or the community.

The change of status is often marked by ceremonial alterations of physical appearance—the shaving or growing of hair, removal of teeth, scarification (facial scarring), and circumcision. Clothing and attire are also key elements. Robes, beads, body piercing, and body paint may all be used to symbolize status or a state of being in transition and so play an important ceremonial role.

Initiations into adulthood, and its associated role of warrior, commonly involve trials of bravery and endurance. Circumcision, in particular, is widely practiced and is thought to create, through pain, the quality of bravery that the man will have to rely upon in later life. Initiations are also often the time when secret knowledge is passed on to the younger generation and when youngsters learn how to fend for themselves.

Elaborate birth and death rituals are intimately related to the world of spirits. Earthly life is often seen as only one phase in the existence of spirits. Babies and young children may not be considered fully human until their spirits have occupied their bodies. Ceremonies are held to encourage this process, or to protect the child during the transitional phase. Naming ceremonies are often delayed until the child's survival looks certain, at which point they serve to incorporate the child into the community of the living. On death the spirits of the dead may create problems for the living, and so elaborate ceremonies are held to ease the passage of the spirit and ensure its happiness.

Today, many life-cycle rituals are still practiced despite the spread of Christian and Islamic values. Often such rites are practiced alongside Christian and Islamic ceremonies, and they are seen as complementing rather than contradicting the new faith. One major change, however, is that ceremonies involving potentially dangerous body modifications, such as circumcision, are now increasingly being carried out in sterile hospital environments. There is pressure to ban the controversial practice of female circumcision. This practice is often known as female genital mutilation, and can be very harmful to a girl's health and future sexual activity.

In this life-cycle ritual held by the Ethiopian Church, a girl is immersed in a pool to purify her and increase her fertility.

NONRELIGIOUS FESTIVALS

Today a wide variety of secular festivals exists throughout East Africa. Many of these are of modern origin. Kenya plays host to festivals as diverse as the Maralal International Camel Derby and Festival and the Mombasa Carnival. The Tanzanian island of Zanzibar holds the Indian Ocean Dhow (sailing boat) Festival and the Sauti za Busara ("Sounds of Wisdom") Swahili Music Festival. In Ethiopia the many festivals celebrated in Christian and Islamic calendars are held alongside several secular (nonreligious) festivals, including Patriots' Day and a celebration marking the overthrow of the hated Marxist regime, the Derg, in 1991.

Many countries in the region also hold film, art and book festivals. Prominent annual movie events are the Zanzibar International Film Festival and the Amakula Kampala Festival. On a more solemn note, April 2004 saw a week of remembrance in Rwanda to honor the victims of the genocide there ten years before.

SEE ALSO: *Christianity; English-language literature; Islam; Movies; Music and musical instruments; Oral literature.*

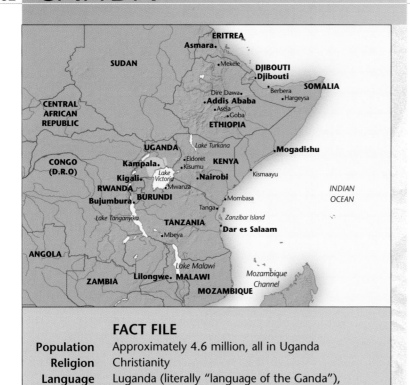

FACT FILE

Population	Approximately 4.6 million, all in Uganda
Religion	Christianity
Language	Luganda (literally "language of the Ganda"), some English.

TIMELINE

c.1100	Creation of Bunyoro–Kitara kingdom.
1500	Fragmentation of Bunyoro–Kitara into kingdoms of Bunyoro, Buganda, and Ankole.
c.1750–1850	Buganda achieves position of regional dominance.
1862	First Europeans, the British explorers John Speke and James Grant arrive at Mutesa's court.
1884	King Mutesa dies and is succeeded by his son Mwanga.
1893	Buganda is declared a British protectorate (colony).
1921	The Bataka Association is formed to protest land allocation under British rule.
1962	Uganda gains independence under Prime Minister Milton Obote. Kabaka Mutesa II is made president.
1966	Obote deposes Kabaka Mutesa II, who flees into exile.
1971	Head of the Ugandan army, Idi Amin Dada, overthrows Obote in a military coup.
1979	Amin is overthrown and Obote reinstalled.
1986	Obote is overthrown by Yoweri Museveni's National Resistance Movement (NRM).
1993	Museveni grants legal recognition to the old Ugandan kingdoms and Mutebi II is crowned 36th Kabaka.

THE GANDA (OR BAGANDA) ARE A BANTU-SPEAKING PEOPLE WHO INHABIT THE REGION TO THE NORTHEAST OF LAKE VICTORIA, IN PRESENT-DAY UGANDA. THEIR FORMER KINGDOM OF BUGANDA HAS RECENTLY BEEN RESTORED IN A CEREMONIAL ROLE.

HISTORY

Bantu speakers probably arrived in the Lake Victoria region some 2,000 years ago. By 1100 C.E. they had created the first of a number of kingdoms known as Bunyoro–Kitara (see NYORO). By the late 15th century this kingdom had fragmented into three different states, including one (known as Buganda) ruled by the Ganda. For some time Buganda was dominated by its neighbor Bunyoro. However, from the mid-18th century on, Buganda began a long campaign of expansion.

In the mid-19th century King Mutesa revolutionized the Bugandan army, creating a standing force with a ranked officer class. These developments meant that Buganda was the foremost power in the region when European travelers and Swahili slave traders began to arrive there in the following decades. The late 1880s saw a wave of missionary activity as British Protestants and French Catholics vied to convert Bugandans. Many Ganda also adopted Islam at this time. In 1890 Mutesa's son and successor Mwanga signed a treaty with the German East Africa Company, only for Germany to cede the territory to British control a few months later.

Following a series of running battles between Mwanga and the British East Africa Company, Britain formally declared Buganda a protectorate in 1894. The king (kabaka) was kept as a figurehead, the Bugandan system of government was extended to cover the entire territory, and Buganda was granted special, semi-independent federal status within the newly formed territory of Uganda. This favorable treatment of Buganda over its historical rivals sowed the seeds of the tensions that were to tear Uganda apart after independence.

In 1993, after Uganda restored its ancient kingdoms, the heir to the Bugandan throne returned from exile to be crowned as Ronald Muwenda Mutebi II. Buganda is a constitutional monarchy, and the Kabaka attends the opening and closing ceremonies of Uganda's parliament each year.

THE KABAKA

The office of the kabaka, the ruler of Buganda, combined both ritual and political functions. As well as being the head of the clan chiefs, the king was entrusted with maintaining the nation's fertility and prosperity. He was the war leader and made the most important sacrifices to the deities and dead kings. Important symbols of kingship included the famous national drums, whose capture was supposed to signify the downfall of the nation, the king's throne (consisting of a wooden chair and a rug of various animal skins), a shield and a spear symbolizing the defense of the nation, and the sacred fire. In 1966 Prime Minister Milton Obote deposed King Mutesa II. However, in 1993 Mutesa's son, Ronald Muwenda Mutebi II, was reinstated in a ceremonial role.

SOCIETY AND DAILY LIFE

Buganda is well watered and fertile, and historically the Ganda have mainly been farmers. The chief crop is the banana (*matoke*; see box feature), of which the Baganda cultivate numerous varieties. Cultivation is predominantly the reserve of women, and husbands are expected to provide their wives with land and hoes to grow food. Maintaining the homestead and looking after cattle were traditionally male roles, though the Baganda keep far fewer cattle than their neighbors. Today many of the divisions between male and female work have broken down.

In the past, the Bugandan king exercised ultimate authority, though the roles of the queen mother and queen sister were also important. In addition, there were 52 clan chiefs under the king, and below them many lineage chiefs. Chiefly positions were not necessarily hereditary, as the lineage elders could choose any of the former chief's close male relatives to succeed him. In theory there was no class structure and any man could rise to a position of authority. The British kept this system of government under their colonial rule, but the privileges of Buganda and the other historical kingdoms were abolished after independence in 1967, and the kabaka fled into exile. Even so, the Baganda constantly remained very influential in government and administration.

RELIGION AND CULTURE

Today most Baganda are Christian, mainly belonging to either the Roman Catholic Church or the Church of Uganda (an offshoot of the Anglican Church). In the past they worshipped various national and clan deities, many of whom were semimythical ancestral figures. Large conical huts or temples were constructed to honor these gods, who often had their own priests. Figurines and amulets, objects thought to hold mystical powers, were also important,

MATOKE

In the Luganda language, *matoke* not only means "banana" but is also the general word for "food," indicating the importance of this crop. Bananas were originally domesticated in Southeast Asia and probably brought to Africa some 2,500 years ago. Today Ugandans consume more bananas per head of population than any other people. In Buganda, the fruit can be divided into three classes: those (*toke*) that are harvested green and used as a staple, those (*mbide*) used to make beer, and those (*gonja*) eaten as a sweet fruit. Different varieties, selected for their qualities, are used for each purpose. Harvesting the bananas is a skilled task, as they must neither be picked when they are under-ripe, nor too late, when they are too sweet. Green bananas are usually peeled, wrapped in the leaves of the plant, and boiled until they are soft.

Buganda includes the Ugandan capital Kampala (top left); yet, amid the skyscrapers, many Ganda still live in shantytowns like the suburb of Kamwokya (below left). This lifestyle contrasts with village life near Jinja (below) in eastern Buganda.

and ritual specialists were employed to make these objects as well as medicines.

The burial sites of the dead kings were greatly revered, and temples were built around them. The dead kings were thought to live in these temples and were venerated in the same way as the national and clan deities. The dead father of the current king was thought to communicate with him during ceremonial visits to the temple and the chief guardian of the temple was the king's sister. Today the Kasubi royal tombs in Kampala are a World Heritage Site.

SEE ALSO: *Architecture; Christianity; Festival and ceremony; Nyoro.*

FACT FILE

Population	Rwanda c.8.4 million (84% Hutu, 15% Tutsi), Burundi c.6.3 million (85% Hutu, 14% Tutsi)
Religion	Christianity (Roman Catholicism)
Language	Kinyarwanda (Rwanda), Kirundi (Burundi)

TIMELINE

1000–1500	Tutsi pastoralists arrive in the area, establishing the kingdoms of Rwanda and Urundi.
c.1600	Rwandan rulers expand and consolidate their rule.
1894–98	German East Africa absorbs Rwanda and Burundi.
1916	During World War I, Belgium seizes Rwanda-Urundi.
1961–62	Hutu majority gain control in Rwanda and abolish Tutsi monarchy. Burundi becomes an independent monarchy.
1966	Michel Micombero seizes power in a coup in Burundi.
1972	200,000 Hutu are killed in a failed coup in Burundi.
1987–88	A coup in Burundi sees thousands of Hutus massacred by Tutsi and a flood of refugees enter southern Rwanda.
1990	Rwanda Patriotic Front (RPF) invades northern Rwanda.
1993	First Hutu president Melchior Ndadaye is elected in Burundi, but assassinated a few months later.
1994	Genocide in Rwanda. The RPF takes power and brings the genocide to an end.
1996	300,000 die in civil war in Burundi.
2002	Burundi conflict ends as Hutus enter government.
2004	Ceremonies mark the 10th anniversary of the genocide.

T HE HUTU AND TUTSI MAKE UP MOST OF THE POPULATION OF BOTH RWANDA AND BURUNDI. THE HISTORIES OF THESE PEOPLES HAVE LONG BEEN INTERTWINED. IN THE MID-1990S, GROWING TENSION BETWEEN THEM ERUPTED INTO ONE OF THE MOST SERIOUS OF MODERN-DAY GENOCIDES—ATTEMPTS TO WIPE OUT A WHOLE PEOPLE.

HISTORY

Ethnically, Rwanda and Burundi are made up of three groups. The first inhabitants of the region were the Twa, who lived a hunting and gathering lifestyle. Then, around 2,000 years ago, the Twa were joined from the west by the agricultural Hutu, who cleared vast areas of forest and confined the Twa to the remaining wooded areas. Sometime before the 15th century a succession of Tutsi cattle herders (pastoralists) migrated into the area, probably from the east in present-day Uganda. They soon dominated the Hutu.

According to the oral histories of the Tutsi-dominated royal court, the Hutu admired the large cattle herds of the Tutsi and readily accepted the establishment of Tutsi royal "Nyiginya" dynasties. In truth, it is more likely that a number of small Hutu states continued to resist Tutsi domination. Yet, up until colonial intervention (first by Germany and, after World War I, by Belgium), the chief powers in the region were the Tutsi kingdoms of Rwanda and Urundi.

The ethnic tensions that came to characterize the relations between the Hutu and Tutsi have their origin in the reign of Rwabugiri (c. 1860–95). He greatly expanded the authority of the Tutsi royal court and introduced the hated feudal labor system known as *uburetwa*. This system forced Hutu peasant farmers to work Tutsi lands for a certain number of days per week.

Social injustice and inequalities were maintained under colonial rule. The Belgian colonial authorities reinforced ethnic distinctions by making everyone carry an identity card listing his or her "race." Until the late 1950s the Belgian administration strongly supported the Tutsi aristocracy, but then under pressure from the Catholic Church and the international community abruptly switched its support to the majority Hutu. The result was that, with the end of colonialism in 1962 Rwanda became an independent republic under Hutu rule, while Burundi remained a monarchy controlled by the Tutsi king (mwami). In both countries, Hutu–Tutsi violence soon broke out. In particular, an unsuccessful attempt by the Hutu to overthrow the Tutsi elite in Burundi in 1972 resulted in major bloodshed.

THE RWANDAN GENOCIDE

In 1986, Tutsi refugees in western Uganda formed the Rwandan Patriotic Front (RPF) to overthrow the Hutu government of Rwanda. After seven years of guerrilla activity, the two sides signed a cease-fire and power-sharing agreement in 1993. However, Hutu and Tutsi extremists prevented this peace from being implemented. In particular, Hutu hardliners in the Rwandan military began to train and arm Hutu militias called the Interahamwe ("those who stand together"). In early April 1994 an airplane carrying the Hutu presidents of both Rwanda and Burundi was shot down near Kigali, killing both men. The act was immediately blamed on the Tutsi and, whipped up by hate propaganda broadcast on Hutu radio, the Interahamwe and the Rwandan military began massacring Tutsis and moderate Hutus. The United Nations had a small force present in Rwanda to oversee the 1993 peace accord, but it was withdrawn after being attacked, rather than strengthened. Accordingly, the Interahamwe were left to kill without restraint. In the three months before the RPF was able to capture Kigali some 800,000 Rwandans were slaughtered.

A Hutu village in Burundi with traditional reed and grass dwellings; each village is made up of around 20 fenced compounds.

Tutsi wearing leopardskin cloaks and flowing headdresses and carrying spears perform the "Ntore" dance. This coordinated drilling dance performed by young men reflects the Tutsi warrior tradition.

DANCE AND RECONCILIATION
The dance group Ballet National du Rwanda was formed in 1974, and it specialized in preserving folklore elements of the nation's cultural tradition. The project was instigated by the then-president Juvenal Habyarimana (one of the two leaders killed in the aircrash that sparked the 1994 genocide). The company gained international recognition for its performances in the late 1980s and had around 200 members. Following the massacres of 1994, ballet director Jules Musasizi and the group are helping to bring about reconciliation between Rwanda's communities, performing at festivals throughout the country.

SOCIETY AND DAILY LIFE
Since the 1994 genocide, life for most Rwandans has undergone a great change. Despite the legacy of terrible bitterness, the old divisions between Hutu and Tutsi are being broken down. The process of reconciliation between the two communities is being hailed as an international success story. Even prior to the genocide the traditional distinction between cattle-keeping Tutsi and agricultural Hutu was difficult to justify, since both Hutu and Tutsi were engaged in a wide range of occupations.

Today, the majority of both peoples are still farmers, growing sorghum, millet, corn, and bananas and keeping some livestock. Although the HIV/AIDS epidemic is a

serious problem, levels of literacy are improving and primary education has become universally available. Today Rwanda seems firmly set on the road toward becoming a modern society based on individual merit rather than divisive tribalism. In Burundi moves toward peace are occurring at pace and there is a great hope that the country will be able to follow in the footsteps of its neighbor.

RELIGION AND CULTURE

Today most Hutu and Tutsi are Christian; Roman Catholicism is particularly strong. However, the Catholic Church has been severely criticized for its role in emphasizing ethnic divisions in the years running up to the Rwandan genocide. Some Hutu and Tutsi still follow preexisting beliefs, worshipping a benevolent creator god known as Imana. Attention is also paid in Hutu and Tutsi beliefs to the spirits of ancestors. Offerings are made to the ancestors at family shrines to ensure the continued well-being of the living.

The Hutu make baskets, carve craftworks from wood, and forge iron implements, including a characteristic long-handled curved knife to cut fruit from trees. The Tutsi are known for their basketmaking and their ornamental screens.

SEE ALSO: *Christianity; Festival and ceremony; Television and radio.*

Rwandans at a refugee camp in 1994. The terrible violence that swept Rwanda and Burundi in the mid-1990s was the worst attempt at "ethnic cleansing" since World War II. Yet the Hutu and Tutsi are very similar, and many people regard the divisions that led to this conflict as based on class and economic factors rather than ethnic differences. These divisions were solidified during the colonial era.

TIMELINE

615	Kingdom of Axum offers refuge to Muslims fleeing persecution in Mecca. Muslim communities subsequently flourish along the coast of Eritrea.
780	First wooden mosque on the Swahili coast at Shanga on the Lamu archipelago, Kenya.
900–1000	Creation of the first Swahili towns with stone mosques, Arabic literacy and currency based on Near Eastern Islamic standards.
1400–1500	Emergence of Sufi orders in Somalia.
1500	Sultanate of Adel in eastern Ethiopia dissolves into a number of smaller states.
c.1540	Series of wars between Christian highland Ethiopia and lowland Muslim states.
1698	Oman takes control of Mombasa from the Portuguese
1832	Sultan of Oman moves his capital to Zanzibar.
1969	Siad Barre seizes power in Somalia and instigates socialist reforms. He initially declares the country to be Islamic but later announces a series of reforms creating a secular state separate from religious control.
1991	Siad Barre is overthrown; Somalia descends into civil war.
1992	U.S. marines land near Mogadishu in failed relief mission.
1998	U.S. embassies in Tanzania and Kenya are bombed by Islamist extremist groups linked to al-Qaeda.
1995–2001	Threat of Islamist rule on Zanzibar leads to election rigging and violent protests.

ISLAM FIRST ARRIVED IN EAST AFRICA WITH ARAB TRADERS IN THE MID-SEVENTH CENTURY. MUSLIM COMMUNITIES RAPIDLY ESTABLISHED THEMSELVES ALONG THE SOUTHERN END OF THE RED SEA. BY 1500 ISLAM HAD SPREAD AS FAR AS SOUTHERN TANZANIA.

HISTORY

From its first foothold in the Horn of Africa Islam spread inland into Ethiopia and southward along the Somali and Swahili coasts. Its spread in the north was aided by the migration of Arabs from the Arabian peninsula, while conversion along the Swahili coast came about through trade contacts. Swahili people who converted to Islam enjoyed great advantages, as it placed traders on a more equal footing with their Arabian partners and protected them from enslavement. From the early 17th century on Omani Arabs took control of the East African coast, eventually moving the seat of the Sultanate of Oman to Zanzibar in 1832. Omani rule confirmed the strong Islamic flavor of the coast, which remains to this day.

ISLAM TODAY

Today Islam is the dominant religion in Djibouti, Somalia, and along the Indian Ocean coast as far south as northern Mozambique. Islam is also widespread throughout the highlands, and northwestern and eastern lowlands, of Ethiopia, while Muslims make up around half of the population of Eritrea. Isolated Muslim populations also exist throughout the region, particularly in urban centers, although these are relatively recent migrants.

A mosque in Djibouti, a small country on the Horn of Africa. This region witnessed the introduction of Islam into East Africa, from where it rapidly spread down the Indian Ocean coast.

Most East African Muslims are Sunni and generally adhere strictly to Islamic principles. However, non-Islamic beliefs still form an important part of people's daily lives among some Muslim groups. The Swahili continue to distinguish between orthodox Islamic practices (*dini*) and local traditions and customs (*mila*), such as sacrifice and the veneration of ancestors. Islam in Swahili society has always been uniquely African, as clearly displayed in its architectural styles.

In Somalia the 1969 revolution introduced reforms that reduced the role of Islam in the state. This sparked a series of conflicts that eventually led to the overthrow of President Said Barre in 1991. Since the start of its civil war, Islamist extremism has increased in Somalia. Traditional Islam in Somali has a strong emphasis on Sufi mysticism and members of the Sufi orders, known as dervishes, commonly traveled the country, teaching and asking for alms.

SPIRIT POSSESSION AND ISLAM

Many of the Giriama people who live on the coastal lowlands of Kenya near Mombasa have converted to Islam, as it enables them to trade with other Kenyan Muslims on a more equal basis. However, since the Giriama retain many preexisting beliefs, such as communicating with ancestors and spirits, their conversion has to accommodate ideas of spirit possession acceptable to both traditions: Giriama converts resolve this dilemma by claiming to be possessed by an Islamic spirit. Spirit possession is also common among Muslim women across the region. In the Zar cult that has emerged, women are possessed by certain spirits that might allow them to challenge aspects of male domination such as codes of dress and seclusion, and problems of divorce following infertility.

SEE ALSO: Architecture; Christianity; Festival and ceremony; Somali; Swahili.

Muslims celebrate the birthday of the prophet Muhammad (a festival called Mawlid an-Nabi) at a mosque in Stone Town on the island of Zanzibar. This celebration is held throughout the Islamic world, and involves processions and the narrating of stories about the prophet's life.

KALENJIN

FACT FILE

Population	Around 4 million mostly in Kenya (a few pastoral Pokot live seasonally in Uganda)
Religion	Christianity, preexisting practices
Language	The Kalenjin languages form the branch of Nilotic known as Southern or Highland Nilotic. Kalenjin dialects are not mutually intelligible and Pokot, in particular, is highly distinct. Most Kalenjin speak Swahili, and English is now also widely used.

TIMELINE

c.1000	Early Kalenjin peoples migrate south into western Kenya.
c.1600–1700	Maasai push into Sirikwa territory in the Rift and on Uasin Gishu. Sirikwa probably break up at around this time, giving rise to modern Kalenjin groups.
c.1700	The Kalenjin build irrigation systems along the western escarpment of the Rift Valley north of Baringo.
1888	British East Africa Company begins conquest of Kenya, building trading forts inland from Mombasa.
1895–1901	Construction of the Uganda Railway. White settlers enter the Kenyan highlands, sparking the Nandi wars.
1952	Start of Mau Mau (mainly Kikuyu) uprising in Kenya.
1963	Kenya wins independence from Britain.
1978	Daniel Arap Moi, a Tugen, becomes Kenya's second president.
2002	Moi leaves office and Mwai Kibaki, a Kikuyu, becomes president.
2004	Pokot and Marakwet involved in ongoing ethnic clashes.

SEVERAL ETHNIC GROUPS LIVING IN AND AROUND KENYA'S WESTERN HIGHLANDS ARE KNOWN COLLECTIVELY AS THE KALENJIN. THEY INCLUDE THE NANDI, KIPSIGIS, ELGEYU, TUGEN, SABEI, MARAKWET, AND POKOT PEOPLES.

HISTORY

The ancestors of the present-day Kalenjin migrated south into western Kenya around 1,000 years ago. They are well known for their pit-settlements (also called Sirikwa holes). These dispersed farming and herding settlements were later disrupted by Maasai migration into the area. Today, the descendants of these settlers are called Kalenjin, but that name was not coined until the 20th century. A radio commentator became well-known for his catchphrase "I tell you!" ("Kalenjin"). The term came to be used for all Highland Nilote speakers.

Between 1895 and 1905 the Nandi clashed with the British, who were building the Mombasa–Uganda railroad. The British duly conquered them and enclosed them in the Nandi Reserve. In more recent years the Kalenjin came to prominence when Daniel Arap Moi—a Tugen—succeeded Jomo Kenyatta as Kenya's second president. The Kalenjin have also produced many of Kenya's famous long- and middle-distance runners.

SOCIETY AND DAILY LIFE

Kalenjin groups mix farming and herding in differing proportions. Many Pokot are committed herders (pastoralists) growing few or no crops, while the Nandi have become more accustomed to settled farming. The Tugen and the Kipsigis, on the other hand, combine agriculture with large-scale stock raising, while the Marakwet are well known for their intensive agriculture based on an elaborate irrigation system.

Pokot women wearing traditional beadwork collars. The women of this group are also known for making gourds into richly decorated storage containers.

RELIGION AND CULTURE

In the past the Kalenjin believed in the existence of a supreme being, who among the Pokot is known as Tororot. Tororot is thought to manifest himself in the form of lightning and is said to inhabit certain caves and high places. While the Kalenjin have a society that is largely based on equality, prophets or religious leaders have sometimes existed. The Pokot adopted religious leaders at times of crisis, while the Nandi were led in their wars against the British by a chief with priestly authority. Today most Kalenjin are Christian, at least in name. Various Christian denominations are represented, including Catholicism, Anglicanism, and the Lutheran Church.

Initiation into an age-set is an extremely important ceremony for most Kalenjin, both male and female. The initiation involves circumcision for both sexes, although there is considerable pressure to end the process of female circumcision (often referred to as female genital mutilation), since it can be especially harmful to a girl's health and future sexual activity. As the ritual continues, increasingly these circumcision operations are being carried out in local hospitals; this reduces the health risk and, for girls, allows for a simplified and less dangerous procedure.

See also: Christianity; Kikuyu; Maasai.

Kalenjin social organization is based on the dual institutions of the clan (a large, male-dominated descent group) and the age-set (a group of people of the same age). Kalenjin law is administered by the *kok*, a gathering of clan elders, while defense is the responsibility of the younger warrior age-sets. Polygyny was once common, but has declined with the spread of Christianity.

AGE-SETS AND INTERETHNIC CONFLICT

Among the Kalenjin, age-sets perform an important function as they cut across clan and lineage divisions and can thus provide an alternative method of resolving conflicts and arguments. Corresponding age-sets from peoples in dispute can meet to exchange views and start diplomacy. There is a pressing need for such systems; the Kalenjin have never been politically unified and so, despite the efforts of colonial and national governments, have had a long history of inter-ethnic conflict. Stock raids and reprisals are common, during which people are often killed. As recently as 2001 a Pokot raid on the Marakwet resulted in the death of some 40 people, including women and children.

KIKUYU

FACT FILE

Population	Around 7.4 million, all in Kenya
Religion	Christianity, Kikuyu religion
Language	Gikuyu is an Eastern Bantu language most closely related to Meru and Kamba of central Kenya.

TIMELINE

c.1500	Kikuyu split from Meru speakers and settle their present-day territories southeast of Mt. Kenya.
c.1700–1800	Period of expansion and migration.
1888	British East Africa Company begins conquest of Kenya, building trading forts inland from Mombasa.
1895–1901	Building of the Mombasa–Uganda railroad brings white settlers to Kenyan highlands. Kikuyu Reserve created.
1921	Kikuyu Central Association (KCA) formed to lobby for land reform and oppose British occupation.
1952–56	Revolt by Mau Mau, an anticolonial guerrilla movement. More than 50,000 Kikuyu imprisoned in camps.
1963	Kenya gains independence, with ex-detainee Jomo Kenyatta as the first prime minister (later president).
1978	Kenyatta dies and is succeeded by Daniel Arap Moi.
1982	Constitutional changes ban all political parties except ruling Kenyan African National Union (KANU).
1991–92	Multiparty politics restored in Kenya.
1998	U.S. embassy in Nairobi bombed by al-Qaeda.
2000	East African Community (EAC; founded 1967, disbanded 1977) revived to improve regional economies.

THE KIKUYU, A BANTU-SPEAKING PEOPLE, HAVE THEIR HOMELAND ON A HIGHLAND PLATEAU IN THE CENTER OF KENYA. AS KENYA'S LARGEST ETHNIC GROUP, THEY HAVE PLAYED A MAJOR ROLE IN THE COUNTRY'S POLITICAL LIFE AFTER INDEPENDENCE.

HISTORY

The Kikuyu may be descendants of the first early Iron Age peoples who arrived in the Great Rift Valley some 2,000 years ago. However, a distinct Kikuyu identity can only be traced back to the 16th century, when they split from their close Meru relatives and migrated into their present location on the central plateau of Kenya. Occupying the fertile agricultural lands around Mt. Kenya, the Kikuyu were badly affected by white settlement of the Kenyan Highlands in the colonial period. Forced from their land, many became squatters or laborers and the creation of a small Kikuyu Reserve did little to improve matters. As a result, the Kikuyu were among the first people in Africa to mount a sustained political challenge to the colonial regime. Beginning in 1952 the Kikuyu instigated the Mau Mau rebellion against the British; by 1963 Kenya had won freedom under its new leader, the Kikuyu Jomo Kenyatta.

SOCIETY AND DAILY LIFE

The Kikuyu are predominantly a farming people, though they also keep flocks of sheep and goats. Some herds of cattle are also kept, and are used for bridewealth payments, sacrifices, and feasts.

Kikuyu society is organized around three key institutions. First is the family group (*mbari*, or *nyomba*) which comprises all those related by blood, on the mother's or the father's side. Secondly, there is the clan (*moherega*, or *mwaki*), which brings together several families who can trace their descent from a common ancestor. In the past each clan was administered by a council of elders. Important clan positions include the diviner (*morathi*), and medicine man (*mondo mogo*). Finally, there is the age-set, or *riika*, a group of boys or girls of the same age. The age-sets unite individuals into a strong bond of friendship that provides a mechanism independent of clan or family through which tensions can be resolved.

RELIGION AND CULTURE

In the past the Kikuyu believed in a single creator god known as Ngai. Ngai was thought to live on Mt. Kenya, which is called Kere Ngaya ("Mountain of Mystery") by the Kikuyu. Many Kikuyu still lay out their houses so that the door faces this sacred mountain. The *morathi* are thought to get instructions from Ngai, while clan elders are responsible for making sacrifices of sheep or goats to Ngai so as to ensure rain. As well as a strong belief in Ngai, the Kikuyu also hold the spirits of their dead ancestors in high respect. Illness is often thought to be caused by a displeased ancestral spirit. One of the main functions of the *mondo mogo* is to discover why the spirit is unhappy and bring about a reconciliation.

MAU MAU

In the early 20th century, during the colonial era, many Kenyans were forcibly evicted from their farmland to make way for white settlers and moved to overcrowded reserves. High taxation and low wages kept most Kenyan people in poverty. In 1944, activists formed the Kenyan African Union (KAU) to fight for social justice and independence. Frustrated by the slow pace of change, some KAU members created the Kenya Land Freedom Fighters—later known as the Mau Mau—and began a guerrilla war against the British. In 1952 a huge crackdown began against the Mau Mau, who were predominantly Kikuyu. Hundreds of people were imprisoned without trial, including future leader Jomo Kenyatta. After four years, the Mau Mau uprising was put down, but colonialism had been weakened and Kenya was set on course for independence.

Young Kikuyu men take part in a dance that accompanies the circumcision rite by which they are initiated into adulthood.

Today, although many Kikuyu have embraced Christianity, preexisting beliefs continue to shape Kikuyu life. In the 1920s and 1930s many religious sects arose that mixed Kikuyu and Christian beliefs. Many of these groups have now drawn closer to mainstream Christianity, but Kikuyu Christianity still has a very African flavor.

SEE ALSO: *Christianity; Dance and song; Festival and ceremony; Maasai; Marriage and the family.*

FACT FILE

Population	4.4 million in Kenya; small populations in Uganda and Tanzania
Religion	Christianity, preexisting practices
Language	Dholuo, English.

TIMELINE

1200	Luo-speaking groups begin migrating south.
1500	The Luo settle in Bunyoro–Kitara.
1600	The Luo begin to colonize the Nyanza region of Kenya on the shores of Lake Turkana.
1888	British East Africa Company begins conquest of Kenya.
1963	Kenya gains independence with Luo leader Oginga Odinga as deputy prime minister.
1966	Odinga splits from ruling Kenyan African National Union KANU party to create the Kenya People's Union (KPU).
1978	Jomo Kenyatta dies; succeeded by Daniel Arap Moi.
1982	Constitutional changes ban all political parties except the ruling KANU. Odinga is implicated in a failed coup and imprisoned.
1991	Odinga founds the Forum for the Restoration of Democracy (FORD). Multiparty democracy resumes.
1992	KANU wins the first democratic elections, with a split opposition and political corruption rife.
1997	Amid claims of vote-rigging KANU again wins election.
2002	A coalition involving the National Democratic Party, of Ralia Odinga, a Luo, defeat KANU. Moi steps down and Mwai Kibaki becomes Kenya's third president.

MOSTLY NOW LIVING IN KENYA, THE LUO ORIGINALLY CAME FROM SUDAN. TODAY, THE LUO ARE ACTIVE IN ALL WALKS OF LIFE IN KENYA, INCLUDING COMMERCE AND POLITICS.

HISTORY

The Western Nilotic-speaking Luo originated in the Eastern Bahr al Ghazal region of southern Sudan. Here they broke away from their close Shilluk relatives and began a long migration south, splitting into numerous groups. Around 1500 a small Luo group settled in Bunyoro-Kitara in Uganda, quickly integrating themselves with local Bantu speakers to establish a ruling dynasty. Thereafter, other Luo-speaking migrants created small states such as Acholi in northern Uganda and Alur in northwest Uganda and the neighboring parts of Congo.

By the mid-16th century other Luo speakers had moved east, settling in eastern Uganda, where they were known as the Padhola. Others moved even farther east, spreading around the shores of Lake Victoria, into what is now Nyanza Province in Kenya, and as far south as northwest Tanzania. Today the Western Nilotic speakers on the shores of Lake Victoria in Kenya, Uganda, and Tanzania are generally called the Luo (or, more correctly, the Joluo). However, many groups scattered widely throughout Uganda and southern Sudan have a similar origin and speak very closely related languages.

SOCIETY AND DAILY LIFE

The Luo are the third largest ethnic group in Kenya (after the Kikuyu and Luyia). From the mainly Luo city of Kisumu on Lake Victoria, they dominate politics in western Kenya. They have played an especially important role in maintaining (or disrupting)

the balance of Kenyan politics. Luo leaders such as Oginga Odinga and his son Ralia are key players in Kenyan political life.

Before their arrival in the Lake Victoria region the Luo were chiefly cattle herders. However, the favorable conditions around the lake encouraged them to take up settled farming and fishing. Cattle are still culturally important to the Luo, who use them for ceremonial sacrifices and as bridewealth.

The Luo comprise 40 separate groups, who are bound by a network of clans and age-sets. In the past, clans were ruled by chiefs known as *ruoth*, who were chosen for their wealth in cattle, wives, and children. Communities were further protected by warriors (*thuondi*) and spiritual leaders called *jabilo*. Today the Luo system of chiefs and subchiefs is fully integrated into the Kenyan local government system.

RELIGION AND CULTURE

Most Luo are now Christian, although many still hold to preexisting beliefs and practices. In the past the Luo believed in a supreme God called Nyasai, and also revered ancestors and ancestral spirits. Unlike many of their neighbors the Luo did not practice

circumcision, but rather removed the lower incisor teeth of male initiates. Today even these practices are rare, though the Luo remain the butt of jokes among other Kenyan peoples for their "boyish" uncircumcised state. Ancient funeral rites are, however, sometimes practiced. These include a long period of mourning, male relatives shaving their heads, and driving cattle herds through the family compound.

SEE ALSO: Ganda; Kikuyu; Music and musical instruments; Swahili.

Luo women harvesting the stems of water hyacinths. This plant, which grows in great abundance in Lake Victoria, is used to make wickerwork craft items, including furniture.

LUO HOMESTEADS

Traditionally the Luo live in large family compounds. Today these are generally hedged, but in the past they were likely also surrounded by stone or earthwork defenses. The gate of the homestead faces west or toward the nearest water source. The size of the homestead depends on the number of wives in the family; the layout is circular with the first wife's hut directly opposite the gate, the second wife's hut to the left of the first, and the third wife's hut to the right of the first, and so on. First sons by each wife build their own huts in the northwest of the compound, while second sons build theirs in the southwest. This strict arrangement reflects Luo views on the order of the world, assigning a clear role to each individual in Luo family life and openly displaying this to outsiders.

MAASAI

FACT FILE

Population	Around 800,000: some 500,000 live in Kenya, with a smaller, related group (the Arusha) in Tanzania
Religion	Maasai religion, Christianity
Language	Maasai and Samburu are closely related Maa languages of the Eastern or Plains Nilotic subgroup.

TIMELINE

c.1000 C.E.	Maa speakers migrate southward into the plains below Lake Turkana in northern Kenya.
c.1700	Maa speakers rapidly spread south from northern Kenya into the Rift Valley and across the Serengeti plains into central Tanzania.
1888	British East Africa Company begins conquest of Kenya, building trading forts inland from Mombasa.
1888–1907	German forces occupy and colonize mainland Tanganyika.
c.1890	Maasai hit by rinderpest, smallpox, and political conflict.
1904–08	Maasai lands in British East Africa are settled by Europeans.
1918	World War I ends, and Tanganyika become a British protectorate (colony).
1963–64	Kenya, and then Tanzania, win independence.
1989	The Maasai are excluded from the Masai Mara game reserve by the Kenya Wildlife Service.
1993	Maasai and Kikuyu clash in Kenya's Rift Valley.
2004	Drought and land shortages lead many Maasai to illegally occupy private ranch land in central Kenya.

BASED IN THE GRASSLANDS OF THE GREAT RIFT VALLEY ON THE KENYA–TANZANIA BORDER, THE MAASAI ARE CATTLE HERDERS. TODAY THEIR WAY OF LIFE IS THREATENED BY LAND SHORTAGE.

HISTORY

Beginning in around 1000 C.E. groups of Maa-speaking animal herders (pastoralists) began moving south from southern Sudan into Kenya and Tanzania. The descendants of these peoples are the present-day Maasai and their close relatives, the Samburu. By the end of the 19th century the Maasai and Samburu occupied territory stretching from Lake Turkana in the north, through the Kenyan highlands and the Rift Valley, to the vast savanna plains of southern Kenya and northern Tanzania. Yet the Maasai could not maintain this strong position for long. The end of the 19th century saw them affected by a series of epidemics; first the cattle disease known as rinderpest wiped out their livestock and then a smallpox outbreak killed many people. Massive infighting then broke out among the Maasai, as different groups raided each other to restore their herds. In the wake of these disasters many Maasai diversified, joining neighboring settled farmers and hunters or moving to the growing city of Nairobi to find paid work. Today the Maasai's greatest problem is access to land. Their population of people and cattle are growing, and they are coming into increasing conflict with government authorities and landowners.

SOCIETY AND DAILY LIFE

The Maasai, who first came into contact with Europeans in 1885, are now widely known through mass tourism. They are often romanticized by outsiders as the model of an African civilization untouched by

all-powerful God Enkai (or Ngai), the husband of the Moon. Enkai uses his power to punish or reward people as they deserve.

The Maasai conduct initiation rituals involving circumcising both boys and girls. Girls are circumcised singly or in small groups just before they are ready to marry; this controversial practice of female genital mutilation (FGM) is painful and harmful. The young women then enter a period of purification, during which they wear black cloaks and paint their faces with white clay. After this they are ready to marry, and adorn themselves with ornate, beaded headdresses. Boys are circumcised in large groups and initiated into an age-set. Great emphasis is placed on circumcision as a test of character and the boys are expected to endure the pain without crying out. After the circumcision the boys leave their family compounds and build their own homestead (*manyatta*) together. They also grow their hair and cover themselves with red clay. When they have completed this initiation ritual, this youngest age-set are known as the *moran*, who act as warriors when needed. A key figure in Maasai society is the *laibon*, who is a prophet and healer and directs ritual ceremonies. The *laibon* also acts as a community diviner.

SEE ALSO: *Christianity; Dance and song; Kikuyu; Metalwork; Swahili.*

modern life. While it is true that the Maasai have resisted certain changes that threaten their culture, they are far from being unaffected by modern developments. Under both colonialism and in the post-independence period, they have lost much territory to ranchers. A decline in big-game wildlife, which once helped maintain the grasslands, has also reduced their grazing land. Today many Maasai now earn a living selling jewelry and other crafts to tourists and allowing paying sightseers to visit their homesteads. Many Maasai are also employed as park rangers or as security guards in major urban centers.

A Maasai moran *herding cattle. These young men are responsible for the herds when they are away from the village in the dry season.*

RELIGION AND CULTURE

Many Maasai have converted to Christianity, but prexisting beliefs are still widespread and strong. The Maasai believe in the one,

THE MAASAI AND THEIR CATTLE

The economy and culture of the rural Maasai are based primarily around their cattle. A Maasai creation myth tells how Enkai made the people first, and then their cattle for their communal use. The Maasai's staple food is milk from their livestock. At times of scarcity, for extra nutrition, this is mixed with cows' blood, obtained by making a small cut in a vein in the animals' necks. It is only on special occasions that cattle are killed and their meat eaten. Yet relying purely on herding is a very short-term and fragile way of life, as was shown by the period of great crisis in the late 19th century. Although the Maasai have some dietary prohibitions against eating certain agricultural produce, they in practice often barter with neighboring farmers for food.

MAKONDE

FACT FILE

Population	The Makonde number around 1,140,000 in Tanzania and 200,000 in Mozambique
Religion	Makonde religion, plus some Christianity and Islam
Language	Makonde, a Central Bantu language of the Yao group, is closely related to Chewa of Malawi and Zambia.

TIMELINE

by 1700 — Arab and Swahili slave traders from the East African coast penetrate farther into the African interior, disrupting the region.

by 1800 — The Makonde settle within their present-day location.

c.1835–82 — The neighboring Nguni make raids into Makondeland.

1866 — Scottish missionary David Livingstone passes the territory of the Makonde people on his journey up the Rovuma River in search of the source of the Nile.

1890 — Makonde territory in Tanganyika comes under the influence of Germany as it begins to colonize the region (as German East Africa).

1918 — Germany loses its African territories after defeat in World War I; Makonde are divided between British Tanganyika and Portuguese East Africa (Mozambique).

1958 — Colonial authorities in Mozambique massacre many Makonde, sparking mass migrations into Tanganyika. Makonde join Mozambique's Frente de Libertação de Moçambique (FRELIMO) independence movement.

1964 — Tanganyika, now independent, unites with the island of Zanzibar to become Tanzania.

1975 — Mozambique gains independence.

THE MAKONDE INHABIT THE LANDS ON EITHER SIDE OF THE ROVUMA RIVER, WHICH FORMS THE BORDER BETWEEN SOUTHERN TANZANIA AND NORTHERN MOZAMBIQUE. THEY ARE KNOWN THROUGHOUT EAST AFRICA FOR THEIR SKILL IN WOODCARVING.

HISTORY

The Makonde are Bantu speakers, who are closely related to the Chewa of Malawi and Zambia. Little is known of their origins, although they are thought to have migrated to their present location around 200 years ago from an area south of Lake Malawi. Colonial rule divided them into two distinct populations. Those to the north of the Rovuma river came first under German and then (after World War I) British control. To the south, in Mozambique, the Portuguese colonists brutally put down uprisings, forcing many Makonde to flee across the border into Tanzania. As a result the Makonde came to play a major part in the formation of the Frente de Libertação de Moçambique (Frelimo) national liberation movement, which was based in Dar es Salaam in Tanzania until it gained control of Mozambique at independence in 1975. Today, Makonde from both sides of the border recognize their common ancestry, although they have gradually diverged both culturally and linguistically.

SOCIETY AND DAILY LIFE

The Makonde are mainly farmers, growing cassava, corn, rice, and sorghum. The soils of the region are generally poor and, after a couple of seasons cultivation, fields must be

In Tanzania, Makonde girls with painted faces perform a dance to accompany the ceremony initiating them into womanhood.

left fallow (unused) for some time. This process (known as shifting cultivation) allows natural vegetation to regrow, which is then burned off, releasing essential nutrients back into the soil. Access to water is also a problem—women may walk great distances to obtain water for the household. Today, the Makonde economy has diversified. In particular, they are famous for their highly valued wooden carved masks. Communities of Makonde craftsmen live in large urban centers such as Dar es Salaam.

SCARING OFF INVADERS

The Rovuma River was long used as a route from the sea to the interior. Arab slave trading caravans and European explorers passed through Makonde territory in the 19th century. The marauding Nguni often skirmished with the Makonde, but their isolation on a highland plateau largely spared them the devastating conflicts and slave raids suffered by neighboring peoples. Invaders may also have been deterred by their fierce reputation and appearance. The faces and bodies of both men and women were deeply scarified (ritual scars), and their teeth were filed to sharp points, sparking rumors that the Makonde ate rats, crocodiles, snakes, and even children! Yet later travelers found them very hospitable.

The Makonde people do not have any overall chiefs. Their society is based more on equality, and they live in small independent villages. Popularly elected village chiefs are the highest political authority.

RELIGION AND CULTURE

The Makonde have been in contact with Muslims from the coast for at least the last two centuries, but have strongly resisted conversion to Islam. Likewise, the first Christian mission was only established in Makonde territory in 1924. While Christianity is becoming increasingly common, particularly among urban populations, the Makonde have not converted to Christianity en masse.

Preexisting beliefs remain widespread and center on cults dedicated to honoring the spirits of the ancestors. Makonde masks and carvings play an important role within this belief system as they depict the relationships between the world of the living and the dead. Masks, in particular, are associated with the important "mapico" male initiation dance and were traditionally thought to be very powerful. Today, much of the key spiritual meaning of Makonde carvings has been lost in the growing demand for craft goods catering to the tourist market.

SEE ALSO: Christianity; Festival and ceremony; Islam; Sculpture; Swahili.

MARRIAGE AND THE FAMILY

	Birth rate/ 1,000 population*	Infant mortality Deaths/1,000 births*	Fertility rate: Children born/woman (2005 est.)	HIV/AIDS in 2003 Living with (est.)	Deaths from HIV/ AIDS in 2003 (est.)
Burundi	40	69	5.8	250,000	25,000
Ethiopia	39	95	5.3	1.5 m	120,000
Eritrea	39	75	5.6	60,000	6,300
Kenya	40	61	5.0	1.2 m	150,000
Rwanda	41	91	5.5	250,000	22,000
Somalia	46	117	6.9	43,000	NA
Tanzania	38	99	5.0	1.6 m	160,000
Uganda	47	68	6.8	530,000	78,000

* per annum (2005 estimate)

Accompanied by members of her extended family, a Karamojong woman carries food to her village in northern Uganda. This is part of the **Agentun** *ceremony, which will complete her marriage. The Karamojong are one of several East African peoples who use cattle as bridewealth payments.*

CHRISTIANITY AND ISLAM EXERT A GREAT INFLUENCE OVER MARRIAGE RITES AND CUSTOMS IN EAST AFRICA. YET MANY PEOPLES STILL OBSERVE PRACTICES THAT ARE DESIGNED TO PROMOTE THE TRADITIONAL EXTENDED FAMILY.

Throughout East Africa the term *family* may mean either the basic family unit (a man, his wife—or wives—and their children) or the extended family. Extended families are generally thought of in terms of lineages (people descending from a common ancestor). A larger unit is the clan, made up of a number of lineages united by descent from a common (sometimes legendary) ancestor. Beyond this, kingdoms unite a number of clans under a single ruler. The kingdom of Buganda, for example, comprises 52 clans, each made up of many lineages.

Descent in East Africa is most commonly traced through the male line (patrilineal). However, descent through the female line is also important and individuals may often turn to their maternal relatives for support. When descent is traced through the female line, lineages are termed matrilineal. This does not result in family groups being headed by women, but does make for stronger ties between brothers and sisters. For example, among the matrilineal Kaguru of central Tanzania the ideal family unit comprises a man, his sister, and her children.

MARRIAGE

Throughout the region success and prestige are often gauged in terms of wealth in human resources. Women are praised for being successful mothers, while men aim to gain dependents. Extended families often invest in cattle which are, in turn, used to acquire wives (and hence children). This increases the size of the lineage, its future productive potential, and its prestige. The payment of bridewealth, usually in the form of livestock, compensates the family of the bride for their loss of her labor and legitimizes the claim of the father's lineage over the children of the union. The marriage rite thus consolidates the position and role of children in the community and ensures the continuity of the lineage. It is arguably a naïve, Western view to regard bridewealth payments as "buying" a bride, and therefore as degrading women. Rather, such payments serve vital, community-building, functions.

The marriage rite also entitles children to make claims on the lineage. Lineage members can rely on its protection and support. For example, the extended family provides bridewealth for men to marry. Wives too can expect support from their adopted lineage and gain great influence as mothers of sons. Although divorce is allowed when mistreatment has been proven, the complexity of marriage payments usually ensures that both families have a major stake in ensuring that the marriage succeeds.

The spread of Christianity throughout the region has resulted in the decline of polygyny (the practice of taking more than one wife). Yet bridewealth payments remain common, even among Christian converts.

Generally, individuals are not permitted to marry within their immediate descent groups. Most East African Muslims follow Islamic marriage preferences and ideally practice cross-cousin marriage.

MALE AND FEMALE ROLES

African families are often seen as male-dominated and oppressive toward women. While there may be some truth in this (as in most societies), the roles of men and women within the East African family can also be seen as unequal but complimentary. Since labor is usually divided between male and female roles, this can enable women to gain considerable control over household

GUMUZ SISTER EXCHANGE

A unique form of bridewealth payment is practiced by the Gumuz of southwest Ethiopia. Gumuz marriage involves the direct exchange of sisters between lineages: a man can only marry if a woman, either a sister or a close relative, can be offered for marriage into the other lineage in return. This means that very close alliances are formed between lineages and ensures that both marriages have full community support. Since outsiders cannot buy into the Gumuz marriage system (as they would be able to in more customary bridewealth systems) the Gumuz have managed to maintain their distinct cultural identity.

production and consumption. In recent years, more women have become empowered through having access to goods, such as vegetables and beer, that they can sell. They thus become more fully engaged in modern commercial life. In addition, women's authority grows over time as they become mothers. Most East African societies set great store by the respect that a son (even when adult) should show to his mother. Mothers therefore often wield great influence over their male offspring. As these men become influential members of the community so the authority and respect for the mother also grows.

SEE ALSO: Christianity; Islam; Festival and ceremony.

A Christian wedding ceremony in Uganda. The continuation of traditional practices such as bridewealth in East Africa ensures that marriage is not only a union of two individuals, but also becomes a binding contract between two extended families.

METALWORK

THE ORIGINS OF METALLURGY (METALWORKING) IN EAST AFRICA ARE UNCLEAR. PEOPLE IN THE ANCIENT KINGDOM OF AXUM IN HIGHLAND ETHIOPIA WERE CERTAINLY PRODUCING IRON BY AROUND 300 B.C.E. AS THEIR CRAFT SPREAD AND DEVELOPED, METALWORKERS TOOK ON A SPECIAL ROLE IN THEIR COMMUNITIES, OFTEN BEING RESPECTED AND FEARED IN EQUAL MEASURE.

HISTORY

It is thought that metalworking was introduced into the East African Lakes region in around 300–200 B.C.E. Iron and copper smelting appear to have come into this area at around the same time as one another. Although this fact strongly suggests that metalworking was developed outside the region, local origins should not be ruled out. What is clear is that once metallurgy had established itself in East Africa, a great variety of styles and designs of smelting furnaces soon developed. These took on forms that were quite distinct from those used in Europe and Asia. Furnace types ranged from simple hollows dug into the ground to large slag-tapping and shaft furnaces. Single and multiple tuyères (ceramic blow tubes), with or without bellows, were used to supply air.

Today very few traditional smelters or smiths still practice their art. Mass-produced metals combined with cheap, imported metal tools soon made traditional metalworkers redundant. Some craftsmen still demonstrate their skill in metalwork for the benefit of the tourist trade.

FERTILITY AND POWER

In East Africa the creative process involved in metalworking is often associated with human reproduction. Accordingly, metalworkers are thought to have an influence over fertility both among people and in agriculture. Fear of this potentially

A principal use of fine metalwork was for symbols of royal office. This exquisite golden crown was once owned by the Ethiopian ruler King Menelik II (r. 1889–1913).

dangerous power often meant that communities would impose prohibitions and taboos on metalworkers. Among many peoples the link between smelting and reproductive fertility is made quite explicit. Furnaces are referred to as women and decorated with images of female limbs, breasts, women's clothing, and female scarification marks. When metalworkers in these societies are engaged in smelting, they are also prohibited from having sexual intercourse for fear of ruining the process.

In many societies smelters and metalworkers formed a distinct caste that was forbidden to intermarry with the rest of the community. For example, the Bantu-speaking Sonjo of northwest Tanzania have a special, separate caste in which men work as smelters and their wives as potters. In other societies, such as the Maasai and Samburu, metalworking is seen as a polluting activity that must be conducted outside the *boma* (homestead).

In contrast, some societies revere the powers of metalworkers and symbols of metalworking have even been taken by rulers as insignia of their authority. This was particularly true of the kingdoms of the lakes region in northwest Tanzania, Uganda, Rwanda, and Burundi. In the 18th century, Rwandan kings were buried with large quantities of metal insignia such as spears, staffs, anvils, and hammers. The Karagwe kings were also famous metalworkers who possessed metal "anvils" with down-curved lateral prongs thought to mimic the deliberately curved horns of cattle. These symbols represented the dual status of the king, who was responsible for the fertility of both agricultural crops and livestock, and who also acted as a mediator between the dominant smelting clans and the subordinate cattle-herding clans.

SEE ALSO: *Amhara; Contemporary art; Festival and ceremony; Sculpture.*

HAYA SMELTING

Although their findings have been disputed, some archaeologists have claimed that the Haya people of northwest Tanzania possessed advanced iron-smelting technology. This may have enabled them to produce medium-carbon steel more than 1,500 years ago, many centuries before it was first made in Europe. In common with many East African peoples, the Haya today use cheap, imported metal tools. However, some Haya elders recalled the old techniques and so, together with archaeologists from the University of Florida at Gainesville, they re-created a traditional blast furnace. A cone of mud and slag was built over a shallow pit and was equipped with eight ceramic blast tubes, each connected to a goatskin bellows. The bellows forced preheated air into the furnace, producing temperatures of more than 1,300°C (2,370°F), hot enough to make exceptionally high-quality steel.

This circular knife worn on the wrist of a Dodoth warrior of the Karamojong people is used for cutting meat from hunted animals. Before the advent of firearms in the region, such knives were also employed as weapons.

MOVIES

EAST AFRICAN MOVIES AND MOVIEMAKERS

Title	Date	Director	Country
Pour mieux s'entendre (A Better Understanding)	2002	Jean-Charles L'Ami	Burundi
Keepers of Memory	2004	Eric Kabera	Rwanda
Walking Shadows	2004	Ndungi Githuki	Kenya
Twaomba Amani	2005	Petna Nadaliko Katandolo	Uganda
Stone Town Forum	2005	Farida Nyamachumbe	Tanzania
Sortir de l'abîme (Leaving the Abyss)	2005	Jacques Rutabingwa	Rwanda
The Heart of Kampala	2005	Winnie Gamisha & Andreas Frowein	Uganda
Naliaka Is Going	2005	Albert Wandago	Kenya

An open-air screening of a film during the annual Zanzibar International Film Festival, which has been running since 1998.

ALTHOUGH EAST AFRICA DOES NOT HAVE A LARGE MOVIE INDUSTY PRODUCING MAJOR FEATURE FILMS, IT HAS OFTEN FORMED THE SUBJECT OF FOREIGN MOVIES AND CAPTURED THE IMAGINATION OF CINEMA GOERS THROUGHOUT THE WORLD.

East Africa has not yet developed the type of indigenous film industry seen in other parts of the continent, especially West Africa. While hundreds of small production companies and art-house groups across the region turn out several thousand low-budget drama films each year, the region has never produced a major blockbuster-type film.

Recent films from the region that have been screened at festivals and won acclaim include the Ugandan film *Full of Energy* (2004) by Stephen Nyeko, which tells the story of a village woman who walks out on her unfaithful husband, and Albert Wandago's *Naliaka is Going* (2005), about a Kenyan girl who drops out of school to work as a domestic servant and pay for her brother's college education. In 2005, the renowned Indian director Mira Nair set up the Maisha screenwriters' workshop in Kampala, Uganda, to promote regional moviemaking.

OUT OF (EAST) AFRICA

Nevertheless, East Africa holds a more central place in the international cinematic imagination than any other part of the continent. From the mid-1980s onward, the archetypal African people, landscapes, and even wildlife, of Hollywood cinema have all been East African in origin. Modern cinematic representations of East Africa began with the release of Sydney Pollack's *Out of Africa* in 1985. This movie told the

story of the Danish writer Karen Blixen's life in Kenya before World War I. This nostalgic Oscar-winning film depicted East Africa as an idyllic, "natural" place of harmony. This was contrasted with the destruction brought by European settlers. This basic formula has been repeated many times since, in films such as *White Mischief* (1988), which showed the decadent life led by British settlers in Kenya in World War II and *The Ghost and the Darkness* (1996), about two man-eating lions.

A DARKER SIDE

More recently, the image of East Africa as "Paradise on Earth" has begun to change. Notably, since 2003, several movies have been released commemorating the Rwandan genocide of 1994–95. The most famous of these, *Hotel Rwanda* (2004) tells the story of a Hutu hotel manager who risks his life to protect the lives of his Tutsi guests. Other major films include *Sometimes in April* (2005) and *Shooting Dogs* (2005), which also show the genocide from the perspective of an individual who lives through it.

(Left) A movie poster in the Tigrinya language advertises an adventure film in the Eritrean capital Asmara.

SEE ALSO: *English-language literature; Oral literature; Swahili; Television and radio.*

DOCUMENTARY FILMS IN EAST AFRICA

An up-and-coming form of moviemaking in East Africa is the documentary. Films of this type have the great advantage of being easy to produce and screen, with none of the huge financial investment and distribution deals required for a full-length feature film. They also allow aspiring young moviemakers to display their talent by treating themes of great topical interest in a novel way. The ten-day Amakula Kampala International Film Festival, which began in 2004, provides an important showcase for documentary movies from around the region. Films shown at this event in 2005 included Ndungi Githuki's *Walking Shadows* (2004) on victims of torture under the regime of Daniel Arap Moi in Kenya, Farida Nyamachumbe's *Stone Town Forum* (2005) about Zanzibari children who are passionate about keeping their town clean, and a harrowing documentary following a survivor of the 1994 Rwandan genocide *Sortir de l'abîme* ("Leaving the Abyss"; 2005) by Jacques Rutabingwa.

MAJOR STYLES AND KEY PERFORMERS

Style	Artist	Country
Buganda court music	Evalisto Muyinda	Uganda
Taarab	Malika	Kenya
Benga	D. O. Misiani and Shirati Jazz	Kenya
Dansi	Mlimani Parl Orchestra	Tanzania
Hotel pop	Them Mushrooms	Kenya
Swahili rumba	Simba Wanyika Original	Kenya
Rap	Kwanza Unit	Tanzania

THROUGHOUT EAST AFRICA, MUSIC IS NOT JUST LISTENED TO PASSIVELY BUT FORMS AN INTEGRAL PART OF EVERYDAY LIFE. THIS HOLDS TRUE BOTH FOR THE REGION'S TRADITIONAL MUSIC MAKING AND FOR MODERN MUSICAL FORMS, WHICH EMBRACES INFLUENCES FROM THE MIDDLE EAST, ASIA, AND EUROPE.

MUSIC AND EAST AFRICAN SOCIETY

East Africa is home to one of the most vibrant and diverse musical cultures in the world. Many of its styles and traditions have local origins, while others are adaptations of Middle Eastern, Indian, Central African, and Euro-American forms. These foreign influences were introduced to East Africa over several centuries of contact through trade, migration, and colonialism. Across East Africa, music is not just something that is produced and listened to; it is also part of everyday experience. Live performances are a key part of its vitality. Many people participate in music making—by singing with their friends at home, dancing with neighbors

at a local tearoom, or singing, dancing and, playing instruments as part of religious worship. Music is also an integral part of the general fabric of social life. The central importance of musical experience and sociability is captured in the word *ngoma*. Swahili in origin, the word is widely used throughout East Africa, and refers to music itself (especially music involving some form of rhythmical drumming), to the experience of music—playing it, dancing to it, and the feeling it creates—and to the social contexts within which music is played.

The **krar** *or Eritrean harp is a traditional instrument with five or six strings that makes a mellow, haunting sound.*

LOCAL TRADITIONS

Today the exact origins of most East African musical traditions are lost in the mists of time. However, looking at contemporary uses of music in village settings, it is likely that from the very beginning, most musical styles grew out of, and were embedded in, the routines and rituals of everyday social life. Today, traditional musical instruments such as the Kenyan *nyatiti* (a traditional eight-string lyre), the Tanzanian *zeze* (a type of flat bar-zither), or the Ugandan *akadinda* (xylophone) are most likely to be played during a communal work party, within a

The Drummers of Burundi ("Les Tambourinaires de Burundi") have become famous throughout the world for their energetic rhythmic drumming performances.

THE NYATITI

The Kenyan *nyatiti* is one of many lyrelike instruments made throughout East Africa. It has eight strings that are held on a frame over a cow-skin resonator, and is usually played by a solo male performer. The performance is quite striking, as the player rocks back and forth and sings loudly while playing. He may also wear percussion instruments on his legs, such as metal toe rings or leg rattles (*gara*), and so looks like a "one-man band." The Nyatiti is particularly associated with the Luo-speaking peoples who live around the shores of Lake Victoria. Traditionally, it was used in marriage, initiation, and funeral rites. However, since the 1960s, it has been particularly associated with Benga music.

The Kenyan singer Eric Wainaina is one of the leading lights of new Kenyan music, which blends Benga rhythms and Western styles. His 2001 hit "Nchi ya Kitu Kidogo" attacked government corruption.

religious ceremony, or as part of funeral rites. Drums and other percussion instruments are used to mark time, to raise alarms, or simply to entertain social gatherings. One of the most famous East African musical traditions, Taarab (or Tarabu), was originally associated with wedding ceremonies. Taarab is a form of Swahili poetry set to music. Although it was originally Islamic, it has diversified greatly over the course of the 20th century. Taarab is typical of many local traditions, in that it incorporates influences from outside the region with local forms to produce something new. Thus, Taarab bands commonly use instruments from both the Middle East (such as the lutelike oud) and Europe (especially the guitar), combined with local types of percussion. Juma Balo was one of the masters of this style.

Another famous hybrid form is Benga. Benga emerged in the city of Kisumu in the Luo region of Kenya in the late 1960s, and combines dance rhythms with local musical styles (through its use of the *nyatiti*). Other musical traditions are associated with more elevated social settings. For example, Ikinimba is a form of music and dance that was only performed in the palace of the former kings of Rwanda. It focuses on the *inanga*, a local (lyrelike) instrument.

EXTERNAL INFLUENCES

As in most other parts of the world, throughout the 20th century, East Africa also witnessed the widespread popularity of European and American musical forms. One of the first waves of American music to hit East Africa was the Cuban rumba craze, which began in Tanzania in the 1930s. During the 1940s and 1950s, jazz proved particularly popular, as did Country and Western music later. During the 1990s, rap, reggae, and hip-hop became widespread across the region. In addition, the last 10 years have seen a growing influence of Central African styles, in particular the Congolese dance style Lingala. Artists and groups influenced by Congolese music include Orchestra Virunga and Vundumuna. As with earlier imports, these more recent external influences usually became blended with local styles to create something quite new. Accordingly, Ethiopian musicians produced a distinctive type of jazz known as Ethio-jazz. During the 1960s and 1970s, Kenyan bands developed their own take on Western popular music, while Eritrean musicians even forged a homegrown brand of psychedelic rock.

New styles were also shaped by the social settings in which they were performed. The dance halls that sprang up throughout Tanzania in the years after independence gave rise to a distinctive style of popular music called Dansi. A major band performing this type of music in the 1980s was Mlimani Park Orchestra. Meanwhile the hotel settings of many Kenyan concerts during the 1980s led to the growth of Hotel Pop (also called Tourist Pop). The main exponents of this style are the groups Them Mushrooms and Safari Sound.

A more homegrown style throughout the 1970s and 1980s developed among the dominant Kikuyu community of Kenya. Leading Kikuyu pop artists were Joseph Kamaru and Daniel "DK" Kamau.

SUKUMA DANCE COMPETITIONS

Perhaps the most striking musical events in all of East Africa are the dance festivals that take place each year between June and August among the Sukuma people of northwest Tanzania. The festivals—extremely colorful affairs for which participants spend months preparing costumes—last for between one day and two weeks, and can be so large that they fill a whole sports stadium. Dancers compete for fame and prestige, both for themselves and for their dance society (all dancers throughout Sukumaland are associated with one of two dance societies, the Bagiika and the Bulabo). Although the festivals are mainly about having fun, they also have a serious side. For example, songs performed may contain health messages, such as advice on how to avoid contracting HIV/AIDS.

THE CONTEMPORARY SCENE

The influence of foreign music styles has increased since the 1990s, as new commercial radio and television stations mushroomed in East Africa. Some people regard this as a negative example of globalization. Yet this ignores the fact that many outside styles have been fused with local forms to produce something entirely new. Thus, the last 10 years has seen the emergence of a uniquely Tanzanian form of rap (performed by bands such as Kwanza Unit), a peculiarly Rwandan type of ragga, and a Kenyan style of hip-hop (performed by stars like Shadz O' Black and the Kikuyu rapper Hardstone).

SEE ALSO: Dance and song; Festival and ceremony; Kikuyu; Luo; Swahili; Television and radio.

THE NDERE TROUPE

The Ndere Troupe is a group of cultural performers based in Kampala, Uganda. Taking its name from the traditional Ugandan notched-flute, the endere, the troupe includes performers from all of the country's ethnic groups. As well as keeping alive the musical heritage of all Ugandan communities, the Troupe also aims to bridge ethnic divisions and forge a sense of national unity. This is not a simple project in a country that has experienced several decades of ethnic conflict and divisiveness, and their performances sometimes received an uncomfortable response from local audiences. Yet it is an example of the potential power of music, given how deeply embedded musical experience is in East African society.

NYAMWEZI

FACT FILE

Population	1.2 million, all in Tanzania
Religion	Nyamwezi religion, Islam, Christianity
Language	Bantu belongs to the Sukuma-Nyamwezi language subgroup. It is most closely related to Sukuma, Konongo, Sumbwa and Kimbu.

TIMELINE

2,000 years ago	First Bantu-speaking Iron Age farmers reach central Tanzania.
c.1800	Arab and Swahili trade caravans penetrate the African interior, founding settlements among the Nyamwezi.
c.1880	Nyamwezi begin extensive labor migrations.
1888–1907	German conquest of mainland Tanganyika.
1914–18	In World War I German forces in Tanganyika wage a guerrilla war against British East African troops. At the end of the war Tanganyika falls under British control.
1961	The Tanganyika African National Union (TANU) wins the majority of seats on the Legislative council and independence is granted with TANU leader Julius Nyerere as the country's first president.
1967	President Nyerere issues the Arusha Declaration, leading to villagization and forced resettlement of rural people. Although economically disastrous, it does bring improved education and health care.
1985	Nyerere resigns as Tanzanian president and is replaced by Ali Hassan Mwinyi. Major economic reforms and a multiparty political system are instituted (1992).
1996	Thousands of refugees fleeing the conflict in Burundi enter Tanzania.

THE NYAMWEZI LIVE IN WEST-CENTRAL TANZANIA. THEIR NAME, WHICH MEANS "PEOPLE OF THE MOON," REFERS TO THEIR ORIGINS IN THE WEST, WHERE THE NEW MOON RISES. THEY WERE GREATLY AFFECTED BY TANZANIA'S VILLAGIZATION PROGRAM IN THE 1970S.

HISTORY

The origins of the Nyamwezi are not well known. They may be descendants of the Bantu-speaking peoples that have inhabited the region for some 2,000 years. The Nyamwezi are well known for absorbing many other peoples, and modern Nyamwezi civilization represents a mixture of peoples and cultures. During the 19th century they came into close contact with Arab and Swahili slave traders from the coast. Although several Nyamwezi groups resisted them, many thousands of others joined the caravans as traders or porters and traveled widely throughout the region.

African peoples, many Nyamwezi have left their homeland in search of paid work on sisal estates, cotton plantations, coastal clove plantations, and in cities.

In the past Nyamwezi social organization was based on a number of chiefly lineages. Chiefs were seen as the spiritual owners of the land, who controlled its fertility. The Nyamwezi were divided into as many as 30 independent chiefdoms with populations of between a few hundred and 70,000. Both German and British colonialists adapted this chieftainship system to their policy of indirect rule, appointing the chiefs as agents of the colonial administration. Although the system was dissolved after independence, chiefs have been allowed to retain a ceremonial role.

SOCIETY AND DAILY LIFE

The Nyamwezi are a mainly agricultural people who rely on crops of millet and corn. Most people use hoes to cultivate their crops, although more recently ox plows and tractors have been introduced. The staple meal (common throughout East Africa) is *bugalli*, a stiff porridge or cake made from corn flour and served with meat and/or a vegetable relish. Since independence many more cash crops have been grown, especially cotton, tobacco, rice, and sunflowers. Large numbers of cattle are also kept. Like most

A health care worker talks to a group of Nyamwezi people in rural Tanzania about the importance of keeping their water supply clean.

RELIGION AND CULTURE

Both Christianity and Islam have found converts among the Nyamwezi. Since Arab slave traders founded many of Tanzania's settlements in the 19th century, Islam is common in the major urban centers. Preexisting beliefs are also widespread, focusing on a supreme God, known as Likube, and the veneration of ancestors. The ancestors of chiefs are thought to affect the lives of all the people in their domain, while common people's ancestors only affect their own descendants. Chiefly spirits are believed to have a strong influence over rainfall, and cattle may be sacrificed to appease them. Offerings of grain, beer, porridge, and animals are also made to common spirits at key points in the farming year, at births and marriages, during illnesses, and before making a long journey. Certain non-ancestral spirits such as the *swezi* and *migabo* are also believed to influence the living and are honored by spirit possession cults and societies.

TANZANIAN VILLAGIZATION

Julius Nyerere, president of Tanzania from 1964 to 1985, wanted to develop a uniquely African form of socialism. One key aspect of his plan, which he announced in his 1967 Arusha Declaration, was to reorganize farmland nationwide into a series of state villages (*ujamaa*) acting as agricultural cooperatives. Because the Nyamwezi had always owned land communally, they were quick to adopt this policy. Nationally, however, voluntary conversion was slow, so by 1974 forced villagization was brought in. Like collective farming programs elsewhere, for example the Soviet Union, Tanzanian villagization was an economic failure. Yet it did succeed in bringing health care and education to rural people, giving Tanzania one of the most literate and healthy populations in the region today.

SEE ALSO: Festival and ceremony; Islam; Makonde; Marriage and the family; Swahili.

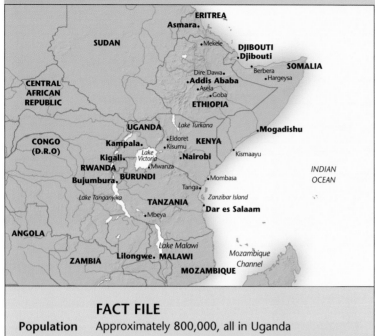

FACT FILE

Population	Approximately 800,000, all in Uganda
Religion	Christianity (Protestant, Catholic), Nyoro religion
Language	Nyoro is a Bantu language of the Nyoro-Ganda group.

TIMELINE

500 B.C.E. First Bantu speakers arrive in the Lake Victoria region.

1100 Creation of Bunyoro–Kitara kingdom.

1500 Fragmentation of Bunyoro–Kitara into the kingdoms of Bunyoro, Buganda, and Ankole.

c.1750–1850 Buganda gains regional dominance over Bunyoro.

1862 British explorers Speke and Grant arrive in Bunyoro.

1869–72 Kabalega comes to the Bunyoro throne and reforms the army, which successfully repels an invasion of British–Egyptian forces under governor Samuel Baker.

1893 Buganda declared a British protectorate.

1899 Kabalega is defeated and Bunyoro annexed by Uganda.

1962 Uganda gains independence with Milton Obote as prime minister.

1966 Obote deposes the monarchs of the Ugandan kingdoms and makes himself president.

1971 Ugandan army commander Idi Amin overthrows Obote.

1979 Amin is overthrown and Obote eventually reinstalled.

1986 Obote is overthrown by Yoweri Museveni's National Resistance Movement (NRM).

1993 Museveni grants legal recognition to the old Ugandan kingdoms and the Bunyoro Omukama is reinstated.

T HE NYORO PEOPLE LIVE IN THE LAKES REGION OF NORTHWESTERN UGANDA. THE KINGDOMS OF THEIR ANCESTORS EXISTED FROM AROUND 1100 UNTIL COLONIAL TIMES.

HISTORY

In medieval times, the Nyoro (or Banyoro) inhabited the kingdom of Bunyoro–Kitara, and then the smaller kingdom of Bunyoro. These states dominated the region until the 15th century, when the rival kingdoms of Buganda and Ankole were established. By the late 17th century Buganda had largely eclipsed Bunyoro. Arab traders from the north began entering Bunyoro in the late 19th century, and were quickly followed by European explorers. Although early British–Egyptian attempts to colonize Bunyoro from the north failed, a new threat soon emerged from the south. In 1893 Buganda signed a treaty that made that kingdom a British protectorate. Supported by the Baganda, the British then launched a new assault on the Bunyoro king (*omukama*) Kabalega, who was finally defeated and exiled in 1899.

SOCIETY AND DAILY LIFE

The landscape of Bunyoro is characterized by areas of raised ground separated by swampy streams. These ridges, known as *mugongo*, have played a large part in determining settlement patterns. Homesteads, comprising one or two adobe houses, are scattered evenly over these areas, each surrounded by its own garden in which bananas (mostly made into beer), millet, sweet potatoes, cassava, and various vegetables are grown. Cotton and tobacco are cultivated as cash crops and provide a reasonable and steady income. Livestock are also widely kept, particularly in the northern savanna regions.

The Nyoro are divided into some 150 clans, membership of which is traced through the male line. Each clan occupies a single *mugongo*, which represents a territorial unit; however, these divisions have become less important in recent years. The ultimate political authority in Bunyoro was once the king, who was responsible for the fertility of the kingdom and was entrusted with its military leadership. In British Uganda the king was retained to rule on behalf of the colonial administration. In 1966 the Ugandan president Milton Obote deposed the Omukama. The monarchy was restored in 1993, but purely to fulfill a ceremonial role.

RELIGION AND CULTURE

Today the Bunyoro are mostly Christian, although preexisting beliefs are still widespread. The creator god of the Nyoro, Ruhanga, is associated with the founding of Bunyoro. Also of great importance are

NTUSI AND BIGO

Oral histories record that a dynasty known as the Bachwezi ruled in Bunyoro–Kitara from around 1350 to 1500, and later kingdoms trace their ancestry to this epoch. Archaeologists who have excavated sites from this period in western Uganda, such as Ntusi and Bigo, have determined that they were thriving settlements with large populations. Alongside many houses, large defensive earthworks have been found. Other features include an *oriembo*, or royal enclosure, and an impressive system of linear ridges and ditches for the protection and watering of cattle herds.

ancestral spirits who can cause misfortune to both the nation and the individual. When the king held political authority, he was also expected to perform sacrifices and rituals to ensure the wellbeing of the kingdom. The kingdom also had a great number of ritual specialists, including rainmakers and spirit mediums.

SEE ALSO: *Ganda; Turkana and Karamojong.*

A group of Nyoro girls preparing to perform a ceremonial dance in the city of Gulu, northwestern Uganda.

EXAMPLES OF ORAL LITERATURE

The Swahili of the East African coast tell the tale of the hero **Liyongo Fumo** (see also AFRICAN-LANGUAGE LITERATURE), who was defeated by malicious intrigue. In one version, Liyongo can be wounded only with a copper knife; in another a needle driven into his navel kills him.

The **Kikuyu** of Kenya trace their origins to a person of the same name, who lived in a village of the same name on the slopes of Mount Kenya. *Kikuyu* means "fig tree" in Gikuyu and is a symbol of fertility, and Kikuyu's nine daughters became the ancestral mothers of the nine major clans of this people

The origin of **elephants** is told in a myth of the Kenyan Kamba people. A magician gave a poor man who wanted to grow rich a potion and told him to rub it on his wife's upper teeth. They duly grew into ivory tusks, which he sold at great profit. But when he tried a second time, his wife grew huge and gray with wrinkled skin and ran off to live in the forest. This explains why elephants are as clever as people.

MOST EAST AFRICAN PEOPLES HAVE MYTHS RECOUNTING THEIR ORIGINS AND THE KEY EVENTS THAT HAVE SHAPED THEIR SOCIETY. TALES THAT EXPLORE THE RELATIONSHIP BETWEEN HUMANS AND NATURE ARE ALSO COMMON.

ORAL HISTORY

Societies worldwide possess a rich store of myths and legends. These comprise stories that are commonly known and are so old that they were first recounted by word of mouth. In literate societies such stories have been familiar for so long a time in written form that it is impossible to unpick which elements were originally spoken and which have been added later by writers. However, in nonliterate societies oral storytelling remains the most important way of passing the wisdom and history of a community down from generation to generation.

Some oral history may have no basis in fact, but can still play an important role by imparting vital knowledge about appropriate social behavior. Storytelling can also be used to pass on key survival skills, describing the nature of the local landscape and the characteristics of its plants and animals. Other oral traditions may draw on real historical events and, while they cannot necessarily be taken as truthful at face value, they can be a highly useful source of information about a group's past.

ORIGIN MYTHS

Origin or creation myths can often be tallied with archaeological, linguistic, and family-tree information to reconstruct the history of a people. For example, each of the Bantu kingdoms in the Lake Victoria and Lake Albert region tells legends concerning the creation of the Earth, the origins of kingship, how the kingdom came into being, and the exploits of their kings in both war and peace. Over time, this very rich body of mythology was embellished and added to. The kings of important states in the region like Bunyoro and Buganda employed special historians and storytellers whose job was to memorize the events that shaped the kingdom and recount them in an entertaining way at important occasions.

The great similarity between the myths of these various peoples is likely explained by the fact that they all claim ancestry from the Bachwezi dynasty that ruled the Bunyoro–Kitara kingdom from 1350–1500. Although scholars have found it impossible to tally every detail in the myths with hard-and-fast archaeological evidence, it does appear that they are ultimately based on historical truth.

In contrast, the various clans of Somalia all have founding-father myths that relate to their supposed Arabian origins. In this case, however, such origins are rarely supported by any other form of evidence, and so actually tell us more about the current nature of Somali society. In other words, they likely originate from a more recent desire to create links to Arabia and the Prophet Muhammad that are intended to legitimize each clan leader's authority and status.

TALES OF NATURE

Many groups also have tales that attempt to explain the nature of the world around them. These may take the form of simple, amusing anecdotes or may convey important knowledge about how the world works. Such stories often also reinforce common sayings and proverbs in the native language. In other words, they embody the folk wisdom of a people. Throughout the region mythology is not regarded as something exotic and remote, but rather as something that is present in all aspects of everyday life and speech.

The Il-Dorobo, a hunter-gatherer people from Maasailand, possess many oral histories that relate to the nature of their surroundings. One example is the story of the Dikdik (a small antelope species) and the Elephant:

"While out walking in the bush one day the Dikdik stumbled over a large piece of

Mursi warriors from southern Ethiopia listen to one of their community storytellers.

LOOKING FOR COOL GROUND

The Mursi of the Lower Omo valley in south-western Ethiopia possess a rich body of oral history relating to their origins and migrations. The Mursi creation myth recounts how five clans originated at a place called Thaleb. From there they migrated in a counterclockwise direction, absorbing other groups of people. This "origin in movement" myth demonstrates how migration is seen by the Mursi as central to their identity. This idea is summed up in their phrase *kalamo ba lalini*, which means "We are a people looking for cool ground." Mursi oral history speaks of several periods of migration, many of which were associated with droughts and the search for better lands. Using the succession of Mursi age-sets, scholars have put rough dates on these migrations and have tallied them with real droughts known from historical and environmental sources. For example, desertification in the past sparked a series of northward migrations that occurred, according to Mursi oral history, after the initiation of the Kera age-set and before the Yoiya age-set. Based on changing lake and river levels, these migrations can then be approximately dated to the early to mid-1920s. Mursi oral history firstly demonstrates how movement is their common response to crisis. Yet it also shows us how, when combined with other pieces of evidence, oral histories can be used to reconstruct actual historical events.

elephant dung. This made the Dikdik very angry and he decided to get his own back. "As I am so small," he thought, "I cannot inconvenience the elephant in the same way. But if all members of my tribe come and use the same place, then eventually we will make a pile that will trip a passing elephant." This story explains why Dikdik have a common latrine area, and so gives Il-Dorobo hunters essential information for tracking down and ambushing this extremely elusive animal.

SEE ALSO: Amhara; African-language literature; Festival and ceremony; Ganda; Nyoro; Somali.

TIMELINE

1550	The Oromo begin moving northward, coming into conflict with the Ethiopian Empire.
1600–29	Jesuit missionaries gain great influence in Ethiopia before being expelled.
1636	Capital of the Ethiopian Empire moves to Gondar.
1755	On the death of Emperor Iyasu II, Gondar is thrown into turmoil due to rivalries between the Oromo and Tigrayan factions at court.
19th century	The Oromo are converted to Islam.
1889–1913	Amhara ruler Menelik II ascends the Ethiopian throne and colonizes Oromia.
1930	Emperor Haile Selassie comes to the throne.
1974	Ethiopian revolution brings Colonel Mengistu to power, who continues Haile Selassie's oppression of the Oromo.
1975	The Oromo Liberation Front (OLF) is formed in southwest Ethiopia to oppose the Mengistu regime.
1991	Facing major opposition from the Ethiopian People's Revolutionary Democratic Front, Mengistu's rule ends.
2005	The EPRDF, with some Oromo support, wins another term in office, but many Oromo still press for self-rule.

INHABITING A TERRITORY CALLED OROMIA IN SOUTHERN ETHIOPIA AND NORTHERN KENYA, THE OROMO MAKE UP THE LARGEST ETHNIC GROUP IN ETHIOPIA. HOWEVER, THEY HAVE OFTEN BEEN PERSECUTED BY THE RULERS OF THAT COUNTRY.

HISTORY

Often referred to in the past as the Galla (a name they do not use themselves), the Oromo are Cushitic peoples, related to the Cushites who inhabited the Ethiopian highlands in around 3000 B.C.E. The Oromo are thought to have originated in modern day Kenya, from where they began a long migration north into Ethiopia. For two centuries, from 1550 to 1750, the Oromo posed a major threat to the stability of the Christian highlands. This long-running

armed conflict saw Ethiopian emperors form alliances with Catholic Jesuit missionaries, who were supported by well-armed Portuguese forces. However, attempts at Catholic conversion led to popular mass uprisings that expelled the Jesuits and won large territories for the Oromo. After 1636, when the capital of Ethiopia moved to Gondar, the Oromo were gradually absorbed into the court and the political life of the Gondar Empire.

SOCIETY AND DAILY LIFE

The Oromo comprise 12 independent groupings, in addition to related peoples in neighboring Somalia and Kenya who speak Oromo dialects. Over time the Oromo have developed a variety of ways of life. They were originally nomadic cattle herders and feared warriors, but are now largely settled. Their principal crops are sorghum and corn. However, cattle also remain important, not only for the meat and milk they supply to

THE GAADA SYSTEM

For over 500 years, the Oromo have had a democratic system of self-government known as the *gaada*. This system is made up of 11 different grades banded according to age. As each age-set (a group of people all of similar age) passes from one grade to another over their lifetime, their rights and responsibilities change. Once they reach the sixth grade, which is also known as *gaada*, at age 40, they are in a position to administer and govern Oromo society, and hold office for eight years until replaced by the next age-set. Once beyond the *gaada* stage, an age-set becomes advisers for three grades (totaling 24 years) until full retirement at age 72.

Oromo people on their way to market. For many decades, under the rule of both Haile Selassie and Ethiopia's communist regime, the Oromo language and culture were suppressed.

the Oromo's diet; a man's status depends on the size of his herd. The majority of Oromo still live in the country and farm, though some have moved to Ethiopia's cities to find work. The Borana of Kenya still follow a more nomadic lifestyle than most other Oromo, herding cattle and small livestock.

Today the Oromo form the largest ethnic group in Ethiopia, numbering some 30 million people. Alongside the Amhara and the Tigrinya, they dominate Ethiopian political life.

RELIGION AND CULTURE

During the 19th century most Oromo converted to Islam, although around 3 percent are Christian and a significant number still follow pre-Islamic beliefs. The preexisting belief system focuses on a single supreme God known as Waaqa, with feasts and sacrifices conducted in his honor. There is a blending of Islam and traditional beliefs in the Oromo's attitude toward spirits; they believe that objects such as trees, springs, and rocks have a spirit, while the spirits of people, known as *djinn*, can possess living people. While the Oromo mostly observe major Muslim festivals, such as fasting at Ramadan, strict adherence to many other Islamic beliefs varies from region to region.

SEE ALSO: Amhara; Islam.

EXAMPLES OF SCULPTURE FROM EAST AFRICA RANGE FROM THE WOODEN FUNERARY POSTS OF THE MIJIKENDA TO THE SOAPSTONE CARVINGS PRODUCED BY THE KISII. PERHAPS THE MOST FAMOUS AND STRIKING PIECES OF SCULPTURE IN THIS REGION ARE THE ELABORATELY CARVED DOORS MADE BY THE SWAHILI.

WOOD CARVING

In the past, the Mijikenda people who live along the coasts of Kenya, Somalia, and Tanzania used to mark their graves with intricately carved wooden posts. Known as *vigangu*, these objects both honored the dead and helped maintain contact between important ancestors and living male Mijikenda elders. The *vigangu* generally took the form of a flat post carved with zigzag or diamond patterns and surmounted by a disk representing a head, sometimes carved with facial features.

Livestock-herding societies of nomadic or seminomadic peoples are characteristic of East Africa. Such peoples, who include the Samburu, Somali, Karamojong, and Turkana, have a tradition of carving small wooden objects for use in their temporary settlements. Examples of such artifacts are headrests, which are used by young male herder-warriors to protect their elaborate hairstyles while they are sleeping. Made with either two or three legs, they strongly resemble those found in the tombs of ancient Egyptians who lived over more than 4,000 years ago. The headrests may serve as stools during the day; however, these pastoralist people often make purpose-built seats. Most carvers are male, although Turkana women are well-known for producing wooden stools and vessels, such as pots for holding milk.

Elaborately carved wooden entrances to homes and businesses are much in evidence in settlements along the coast of mainland East Africa and on the island of Zanzibar. They are the work of Swahili craftspeople; usually comprising a set of heavy, double doors opening inward from a central bar, plus a richly adorned lintel and doorposts, these doorways indicate a household's wealth and status. The finest examples come from the 18th and 19th centuries, when the prosperity of Swahili merchants was boosted by the lucrative trade in spices and other goods from Zanzibar.

The practice of carving doors was brought to the East African coast by Islamic traders from India and the Persian Gulf, but developed into a distinct regional artform. So important were these doorways in Swahili culture that, when a new house was erected, the door would first be made and sited and then the house built around it.

THE TOURIST ART MARKET

With as many as 2 million Western tourists visiting East Africa each year, the region's tourist art market is one of the largest in the world. It has spawned a multimillion dollar art industry. Some countries, such as Tanzania, have tried to regulate and organize the trade. In 1965, the Tanzanian government set up the National Cottage Industries Corporation to help train and support local artists, in particular those selling to tourists. Other countries, such as Kenya, have allowed the tourist art industry to develop without state intervention. In Kenya, production is today characterized by a complex and chaotic web of home producers, dealers, and various middlemen. These different styles of government are reflected in the quality of the work produced. Contemporary tourist art in Tanzania is generally of a higher standard than that on sale in Kenya.

THE STELAE OF AXUM

The famous monumental obelisks (stelae) of Axum are located in several fields around the site of the old Ethiopian capital. Made from a granitelike rock, the obelisks vary in height and shape, yet are all elaborately carved. The carvings take the form of local architecture of the period (some complete with ornately carved windows and locks). The stelae were probably designed to mimic mausoleums (tombs), and are thought to mark burial sites. In 1937–38, the invading Italian army removed one of the most impressive obelisks to Rome. After a long-running dispute between the Italian and Ethiopian governments, Italy finally agreed to hand back this obelisk and returned the first section in 2005.

SOAPSTONE SCULPTURE

In the Tabaka hills of western Kenya lies a deposit of soapstone, which has given rise to a rich heritage of stone carving among the Kisii (or Gusii) people who live there. The Kisii once sculpted this soft stone (which is also known as steatite) into vessels for eating and drinking. Today, they make a variety of artifacts for the tourist trade. The quarrying, carving, and polishing of the stone are all done by hand. Objects are colored with ink or paint before being sealed with beeswax; their surface is then incised to make designs in the natural color of the soapstone underneath.

AN UNSOLVED PUZZLE

In general, however, sculpture is far less widespread in East Africa than it is elsewhere on the continent. This fact has long puzzled scholars, who have put forward several theories to explain it. The first theory points to the relative lack of trees in this region,

The great stone stelae of Axum are thought to date to around the third century C.E. Only one is still standing; the largest, now fallen, measures 110 feet (34 m). In all, there are 126 such obelisks.

MAKONDE SCULPTURE—THE UJAMAA FORM

The Swahili word *ujamaa* is often translated as "tree of life." However, it has a wide range of senses, and can mean anything, from "family" to "brotherhood" to the general idea of "togetherness." In Makonde sculpture, the *ujamaa* form is a column carved from a single piece of wood, made up of a series of intricately carved individual human figures. The figures are intertwined, and are frequently shown locked together, as if in dance. Each sculpture represents a single family, with the older generations (including the ancestors) at the bottom, the younger generations at the top. The meaning is that each family is in fact a unity, with the elders "holding up" the later generations.

Makonde sculpture is made from a form of African blackwood—or ebony—called *mpingo*, and is produced by a specialist caste of artisans. Among the earliest known forms is a distinctive type of mask that is inscribed with large, zigzag shaped scars on the forehead, cheeks and chin. This style of mask is thought to have been worn by young men during initiation ceremonies. In addition, the early Makonde repertoire included intricately carved stools, walking sticks, and ladle handles. However, during the early years of the 20th century, a further three key forms began to emerge. These highly distinctive types of carving are known locally as *binadamu*, *ujamaa* (see box feature), and *shetani*. *Binadamu* represents the naked human body in outline and abstract form, and is not unlike the Western silhouette. *Ujamaa* involves carving multiple figures into a single stump of wood. The various figures represent all of the members of a single family, both living and dead. Meanwhile, *shetani* depict devils, or spirits, which are often twisted and grotesque in shape. Each of these three styles represents one key aspect of the way in which the Makonde understand human existence, and they have remained remarkably consistent throughout the 20th and 21st centuries. However, from at least the 1960s onward, Makonde craftspeople have concentrated more on making sculptures for the tourist art market than for local use. As a result, the general quality of carvings has diminished.

A Makonde craftsman making a wooden sculpture. The Makonde take the myths and stories of their people as inspiration for their works, producing intricate carvings of spirits, animals, and extended families.

which is dominated by grasslands. Yet this is also the case in some parts of West Africa, which has a rich variety of sculptural traditions. The second theory argues that the pastoralist societies that developed on these savannas had little use for sculpture. The wooden carvings of the Karamojong and other peoples tend to disprove this idea. A third theory claims that the influence of Islam—which does not allow any art that depicts living beings—hampered the development of sculpture. Yet Islam was the prime mover in fostering Swahili carving.

MAKONDE SCULPTURE

The Makonde inhabit a large area of southeastern Tanzania and northern Mozambique. Makonde sculpture originated in the latter area, in the plateau south of the Ruvuma river (which forms part of the border between Tanzania and Mozambique). However, from the beginning of the 20th century, Makonde from Mozambique have migrated into Tanzania in ever increasing numbers, with the result that today, the sculptural style is more associated with Tanzania than with Mozambique.

MODERN SCULPTURE

During the 1940s and 1950s, a distinctive style of modern sculpture grew up among graduates of the renowned School of Fine Arts at Makerere (see CONTEMPORARY ART). Perhaps the most influential sculptor of this period was the Kenyan Gregory Maloba (b.1922). Maloba's early works—including his first ever sculpture, *Death* (1941)—are firmly rooted in a distinctly African way of

This Kenyan carved blackwood mask is adorned with beads cut from Ethiopian amber.

were also characterized by the use of massive, heavy media: wood, bronze, other metals, cement, and terracotta (fired clay). From these materials, Maloba produced many of Uganda's public sculptures, including the country's Independence Monument (1962), which still stands in Kampala today. During the 1960s, this unique hybrid style found recognition within the international modern art movement, at the same time as it was being taken up and developed by several of Maloba's students, including the Zambian Petson Lombe and the Ugandans Rose Kirumira (b.1962) and Francis Nnaggenda (b.1936). Lombe's work is noted for the unique way in which it uses European sculptural forms to express African cultural ideas (especially those relating to religion and the family). Also during the 1960s, members of the Makerere School founded galleries to showcase the new style, such as the famous Paa-ya-Paa Gallery in Nairobi. However, the expansion of the tourist art market tempted many students of modern art to give up serious sculpture in favor of more profitable work. As with the Makonde, this trend has seen a general reduction in the quality of sculpture.

SEE ALSO: *Architecture; Contemporary art; Islam; Makonde.*

looking at life and the human place in the world. For example, in *Death*, the figure of mortality is represented as something dangerous, yet also as something serene and comforting. However, over time, Maloba became increasingly influenced by contemporary Western sculptors (especially the British sculptor Henry Moore) which led him to develop a more hybrid style of work. His later works were a fusion of Western and African forms. These later sculptures

PETSON LOMBE'S "FAMILY"

One of the most gifted students at the Makerere School of Fine Arts during the 1960s was the Zambian Petson Lombe. One of his most famous works is a large concrete sculpture entitled "Family" (1961), which stands in the school's grounds to this day. This sculpture blends a predominantly European form with local elements. It shows a tall adult figure seated in a chair, embracing two smaller standing figures, probably children. All three figures have their arms raised up to heaven, as if in a state of trance. The form of the sculpture recalls Western styles of the same period, while the ecstatic posture of the figures is an African motif.

SOMALI

FACT FILE

Population	Around 15–20 million Somali speakers worldwide, with c.7.3 million in Somalia, 4–5 million in Ethiopia, 250,000 in Djibouti, and 240,000 in Kenya
Religion	Sunni Islam
Language	Somali is an Eastern Cushitic language most closely related to Afar and Oromo.

TIMELINE

600–800	Sultanate of Adel established on Gulf of Aden coast.
1400–1550	Wars between Muslims of the Gulf coast and Christian highland Ethiopia. Sufi orders grow among the Somali.
1875–89	Egypt, France, Britain, and Italy occupy Somali lands.
1946	Djibouti made an overseas territory in the French Union.
1960	British and Italian Somaliland gain independence and merge to form the united republic of Somalia.
1964	War between Ethiopia and Somalia.
1969–70	Muhammad Siad Barre seizes power in Somalia.
1977	Somali invasion of Ethiopia is repelled. French Somaliland gains independence as Djibouti.
1991–95	Opposition clans oust Barre, who flees the country. Somalia declines into tribal conflict. US Marines are deployed on disastrous peacekeeping mission.
2001	Former British Somaliland area declares independence.
2003	Breakaway Somaliland holds democratic presidential elections, but wins no international recognition.
2004	Indian Ocean tsunami hits the Somali coast, killing hundreds and displacing thousands more.

THE SOMALI MAKE UP THE LARGE MAJORITY OF THE POPULATION OF SOMALIA AND ALSO LIVE IN ETHIOPIA, DJIBOUTI, AND KENYA. SOMALIA'S LONG CIVIL WAR (1991–2005) HAS ALSO GIVEN RISE TO LARGE SOMALI REFUGEE COMMUNITIES IN NORTH AMERICA, EUROPE, AND THE NEAR EAST.

HISTORY

The origins of the Somali are uncertain. Oral history claims that they are the product of intermarriages between Arabs who migrated from Yemen across the Red Sea and local African Cushitic speakers. This traditional account of their origins states that by the 10th or 11th centuries the Somali had began to migrate southward, displacing Oromo and Bantu speakers from present-day Somalia and settling in their current location. They converted to Islam between the 11th and 13th centuries. However, some

people now argue that the Somali may have originated farther south before any major Arab settlement, and that claims of Arab descent are relatively recent inventions. In reality, modern-day Somali likely number both Arabs and others among their ancestors.

Whatever their early origins, the Somali are recorded in Ethiopian texts of the early 15th century as a distinct group allied to the Sultanate of Adel, the Islamic state that had existed southwest of the Gulf of Aden since around 700. During the colonial period from the end of the 19th century on, the Somali were divided among a number of imperial territories, such as French Somaliland (now Djibouti), British Somaliland (now the breakaway Somali territory of Somaliland), and Italian Somaliland. In 1960 British and Italian Somaliland gained independence and

THE BATTLE OF MOGADISHU

During 1991–92 Somalia was in a state of crisis, with the disruptions of the civil war causing massive and widespread starvation. The United Nations began relief operations, but was unable to work effectively in the climate of lawlessness. Accordingly, in 1992 the U.N. resolved to deploy a military force in Somalia to try and restore stability in the country. A U.S. Rangers and Delta Force team was dispatched, but planners seriously misjudged the situation. Attempts to arrest militia leaders in 1993 resulted in the infamous Battle of Mogadishu, in which two U.S. helicopters were shot down and troops surrounded by rebel forces (as later dramatized in the 2001 movie "Black Hawk Down"). In the ensuing rescue mission 18 American soldiers died and 79 were wounded, while hundreds of Somali militia were killed. By 1995 all U.S. forces had been withdrawn from Somalia. The country was in chaos until 2004, when a transitional government was formed. The peace, however, remains fragile and it is yet to be seen whether the government can impose any order.

Somali herdsmen tending zebu cattle and camels. In the arid, semidesert terrain of Somalia, camels (one-humped Arabian dromedaries) are vital pack animals, as they can walk for long distances without water. Camels are herded and milked only by men.

were united to form the modern nation of Somalia. The Somali people, however, have never been politically united and the country has been ravaged ever since by fighting between clans run by rival warlords. Violence increased during the rule of Muhammad Siad Barre (1969–91), who led Somalia into a disastrous war against Ethiopia over the disputed Ogaden region. After Barre was ousted the country dissolved into a civil war that still lingers on. The former British Somaliland proclaimed its independence in 2001, but remains unrecognized by other countries, while the northeast now forms the self-governing region of Puntland. No functioning government exists elsewhere.

SOCIETY AND DAILY LIFE

The Somali are mainly nomadic, inhabiting harsh semiarid regions, and relying on their herds of hardy zebu cattle and camels. Competition for grazing and water is fierce and has often been the cause of conflicts between different clans. A number of Somali also practice settled farming, particularly in the Juba valley and the Shebelle regions. In more recent years many Somali have migrated to the urban centers to find work in a variety of jobs. Yet since the breakdown of law and order in 1991, most work opportunities are in the armed gangs that extort money in return for protection. Interestingly, in the absence of any effective government or taxation, telecommunications in the capital Mogadishu are among the most developed in the region. Many people have cellphones and Internet cafes thrive. The ongoing civil war saw many Somali migrate overseas.

The factional clan system that bedevils modern Somali life developed in the 11th to 13th centuries. According to oral legend all Somali are related within a vast family tree. They see themselves as descended from a common founding father, known as Hiil,

and many also claim links to the lineage of the Prophet Muhammad. Today the Somali are divided into six major clans: the Daarood, Digil, Dir, Hawiye, Issaq, and Rhanwayn. Each of these are further split into several smaller clans that act more or less independently.

RELIGION AND CULTURE

The vast majority of Somalis are Sunni Muslim. Somali Islam has a long tradition of Sufi mysticism, and many tariqas (Sufi orders) exist within Somalia. These religious brotherhoods act as centers of Islamic teaching, and during the first half of the 20th century they played a leading role in anticolonial movements.

In more recent decades Somalia has seen the rise of Islamic fundamentalism, including the establishment of strict Sharia courts around Mogadishu. These fundamentalist trends became popular as they offered order and stability amid the disorder of the civil war. Yet many Western authorities identify this trend with Islamist extremism, and regard Somalia as a haven for terrorists. The situation has been aggravated by the 1998 terrorist bombings of the U.S. embassies in neighboring Kenya (Nairobi) and Tanzania (Dar es Salaam), and the 2002 attack on Israeli tourists in the Kenyan coastal city of Mombasa.

SEE ALSO: *Afar; Islam; Oromo.*

(Left) The usual dwelling for nomadic herding peoples in Somalia is a tent made of reeds and brushwood that can be easily dismantled and carried away. Nomad camps are generally inhabited by 5–10 families.

ISLAM AND CUSHITIC BELIEFS

Older, pre-Islamic practices still exist within Somali Islam. They are thought to originate from the ancient Cushitic religion, which was similar to that still practiced by the Borana of northern Kenya. The centerpiece of the Cushitic faith was a sky deity called Waaq—a name that is still used to refer to God among the Oromo, Konso, Elmolo, Rendille, and Somali. Other key elements were sacred trees that Waaq temporarily made his home. The Somali still retain vestiges of this belief in the form of myths that claim that their founding ancestors descended from certain trees.

SWAHILI

FACT FILE

Population	c.770,000 total, including 540,000 in Tanzania, 131,000 in Kenya, and 40,000 in Somalia
Religion	Islam; pre-Islamic local practices
Language	KiSwahili, or Swahili, is an eastern Bantu language.

TIMELINE

c.1 C.E.	Iron Age Bantu speakers settle on East African coast.
9th century	Swahili coast well established as a destination on the Indian Ocean trade routes.
14th century	Stone palace of Husuni Kubwa built at Kilwa.
16th century	Portuguese build forts at Kilwa and Mombasa.
17th century	Omani Arabs oust the Portuguese and take control. The East African slave trade flourishes.
1798	Britain and Oman establish a commercial trade treaty over the East African coast.
1832	Sultan of Oman moves his capital to Zanzibar.
1888	British East Africa Company begins conquest of Kenya, building trading forts from Mombasa inland.
1888–1907	German conquest of mainland Tanganyika.
1890	Zanzibar becomes British Protectorate.
1918	Britain takes control of Tanganyika after World War I.
1963	Zanzibar and Kenya both gain independence.
1964	Zanzibar unites with newly independent Tanganyika to form the republic of Tanzania.
2001	Elections lead to violent uprisings on Zanzibar.

THE NAME *SWAHILI* COMES FROM AN ARABIC WORD MEANING "COASTAL DWELLERS." THE SWAHILI LIVE ON THE COAST OF MAINLAND KENYA AND TANZANIA AND ON OFFSHORE ISLANDS, MOST NOTABLY ZANZIBAR. AS IN THE PAST, MANY SWAHILI ARE STILL ACTIVE IN TRADING, WHILE OTHERS ARE ENGAGED IN FARMING OR FISHING.

HISTORY

The Swahili trace their origins to the first Bantu speaking inhabitants of the East African coast. These Early Iron Age peoples were settled in the area around 2,000 years ago, were characterized by their distinctive pottery known as Tana or Triangular Incised Ware. During the eighth century C.E. Islamic traders from the Arabian peninsula began making regular trips to the East African coast. The result was the gradual intermingling of peoples, the Islamization of the native Bantu-speaking population and the development of a uniquely African urban, trading society (see box feature).

From southern Somalia in the north to northern Mozambique and Madagascar in the south, the Swahili established many stone towns. These settlements became thriving trade centers for exchanging goods that came from the African interior with those transported across the Indian Ocean. African gold, ivory, tortoiseshell, and timber were exported, while ceramics and textiles from Persia and China were favored imports. The Swahili towns such as Malindi and Mombasa in Kenya, and Bagamoyo and Zanzibar in Tanzania, reached their zenith in the 13th–15th centuries. But by far the most exceptional of the old Swahili stone towns is that at Kilwa Island in southern Tanzania. This settlement gained its great prosperity by

WIDESPREAD SWAHILI

Swahili, or KiSwahili ("the language of the Swahili"), is widely spoken throughout East Africa, from Uganda and Somalia to Mozambique and Madagascar. Swahili is also the official language of both Kenya and Tanzania (though English is widely spoken in Kenya). This very broad distribution has its origins in the unique history of the Swahili people. The Swahili have long been great entrepreneurs, and their trading and slaving caravans ventured deep into the East African interior. Often, they would establish semipermanent trading posts. These traders brought their language with them and passed it on to local populations. Later, the colonial and postcolonial governments of Kenya and Tanzania adopted Swahili as a national language because it was so widely understood. Today Swahili is spoken as a pidgin (grammatically simplified) language by many diverse East African peoples, enabling them to communicate with one another.

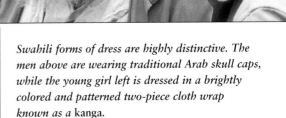

Swahili forms of dress are highly distinctive. The men above are wearing traditional Arab skull caps, while the young girl left is dressed in a brightly colored and patterned two-piece cloth wrap known as a kanga.

controlling the trade in gold from Great Zimbabwe. This funded the building of elaborate palace complexes at Kilwa such as Husuni Kubwa and Songo Mnara.

At the end of the 15th century the Portuguese arrived on the East African coast. Their attempts to take control of the Indian Ocean trading networks effectively killed commercial activity and the Swahili towns went into a long decline. However, from the early 17th century, they experienced a revival as the coast came under Omani Arab control. This was due in large measure to the growth of the East African slave trade,

which witnessed the shipping of up to 70,000 slaves from Zanzibar annually. It was not until the second half of the 19th century that British pressure put an end to this trade, and Zanzibar became a British protectorate in 1890. Yet this island continued to flourish thanks to its export of exotic spices such as saffron, cumin, and cloves. From the early 20th century the Swahili were divided as Britain and Germany founded the colonies of Kenya and Tanganyika on their territories. However, their common history and language ensured that they retained strong

THE SWAHILI—AFRICAN OR ARAB?

When European archaeologists and historians first began to explore East Africa, they were immediately drawn to the great stone towns and ruins of the Swahili coast. The clear Islamic and Arabic influences at these settlements led them to conclude that the Swahili were principally of foreign origin, an outpost of Arabia in Africa. Yet this notion has more recently been challenged by the discovery of many uniquely African characteristics of the Swahili. It has become clear that there is a continuity in the forms of Swahili architecture, ceramics, social organization, and above all in the language, that goes back beyond Arab times. Also, the Swahili are physically indistinguishable from other East African peoples, making it unlikely that any large-scale migration of colonists from the Near East ever radically altered the make-up of the Swahili population. So, although it was fully engaged in the Indian Ocean trade and clearly influenced by the Islamic cultures of Arabia and the Gulf, Swahili civilization was a uniquely African phenomenon conceived, built, and governed by Africans.

The windows, porch, and balcony of this building, the Old Dispensary on Zanzibar (built in 1894), show a mixture of Arab and Indian influences.

links across national boundaries. At the same time, the Swahili display regional diversity, with subgroups including the Bajun, Siyu, Pate, Mvita, Fundi, Shela, Ozi, Vumba, and Amu.

SOCIETY AND DAILY LIFE

The Swahili today are a predominantly rural community who inhabit most of the coast of Kenya, Tanzania, and northern Mozambique. They rely on simple hoe cultivation techniques to grow sorghum, millet, bananas and—following its introduction from the Americas by the Portuguese—corn. They also keep some livestock, such as cattle, sheep, goats, and chickens. Most of the protein in their diet comes from fish and other seafood; there are many fishing communities. The Swahili also prosper in an urban setting, engaging in trade and other commercial activities, and playing an active role in the growing tourist industry.

Swahili society is organized into male-dominated clans, some of which claim Arabic or Persian (Shirazi) descent. Trading activities are based on the *waungwana*—traditional noble merchant families—which are arranged in a strict hierarchy.

RELIGION AND CULTURE

The Swahili have been a predominantly Muslim society for at least the last 1,000 years. However, most combine orthodox Islamic practices (*dini*) with preexisting local customs (*mila*), such as animal sacrificial offerings and veneration of ancestors. In the past, conversion to Islam brought many economic and social benefits, allowing people to trade on an equal basis with the Arab merchants and protecting them from being enslaved. Islam also introduced Arabic literacy and accounting skills, though these skills remained the preserve of an elite. Today the population continues to speak and write in Swahili. The Swahili also adopted certain forms of Arabian architecture, adapting them to local materials and customs. Architectural innovations include exquisite coral masonry (seen especially on Zanzibar), elaborately carved wooden doors, ceramic inlays, and unique pillared tombs.

Today the Swahili are among the most distinctively dressed of Africa's peoples. Men often wear Arab robes and skull caps, or a brightly colored cloth known as a *kikoi* wrapped around their waist. Women dress in brightly colored two-piece wraps called *kangas*, with one worn around the body and the other covering the head and shoulders The floral and geometric patterns of this cloth are often highly ornate and make use of bright reds, yellows, greens, and blues. Swahili proverbs are also often incorporated into the *kanga* design.

SEE ALSO: Architecture; African-language literature; East African Asians; Festival and ceremony; Music and musical instruments; Textiles.

BOTH THE BROADCAST MEDIA OF TELEVISION AND RADIO HAVE UNDERGONE A MAJOR REVOLUTION IN EAST AFRICA SINCE THE EARLY 1990s.

TELEVISION

Television came relatively late to East Africa. Kenya opened its first station in 1959, but most countries did not get television until the 1970s or 1980s. At the outset, and for a long time after most countries had only one national broadcaster, which typically were little more than government mouthpieces. Yet they were also a source of symbolic pride for newly independent nations.

A revolution hit East African broadcasting in the 1990s, as economic reforms forced countries to open up their airwaves to competition. The result was an explosion of new commercial stations. Liberalization also allowed major international cable and satellite operators to gain a foothold. Today, such broadcasters dominate the market.

Most East African families still cannot afford a television set. As a result, TV viewing is generally not a private, domestic affair but a public, group activity. East Africans are most likely to watch television in a crowded bar or hotel, making it a mainly male activity. To cater to this market, broadcasters tend to focus on internationally syndicated sports matches, dance music videos, and action movies (Kung Fu is expecially popular), rather than on, say, homegrown romantic dramas or soap operas.

RADIO

Unlike television, radio is widely available to most East Africans. Practically every household in the region now has access to a radio. The invention of cheap transistor radios in the mid-1950s helped widen ownership. In Tanzania alone, the number of privately owned sets jumped from 70, 000 to almost 2 million between 1960 and 1974. People listen to the radio at home, at work in the fields, in shops and markets, in taxis, and in many other contexts. Public spaces are often marked by a cacophony of competing radio sets. Given the generally low levels of literacy, radio is also the most important medium in the region for communicating news and ideas.

The history of radio broadcasting in East Africa mirrors that of television. Although radio arrived earlier than TV, it too followed the pattern of the single, state-owned broadcaster. However, radio sets could also be tuned to international broadcasters like Voice of America or the BBC World Service.

Radio broadcasting saw the same shake-up as television in the early 1990s. Since then hundreds, or even thousands, of new commercial stations have sprung up across the region, and most locations now have access to dozens of different broadcasters. Some of these new stations have an international focus, while others are national or local in scope.

Broadcast content is extremely diverse. It can range from pure entertainment, such as the latest pop songs, to serious matters like promoting development programs or conflict resolution. Radio has also been used for propaganda, most notoriously by RTLM in Rwanda (see box feature).

RADIO-TELEVISION LIBRE DES MILLE COLLINES

The most infamous radio station in East Africa was Radio Télévision Libre des Milles Collines (RTLM). On air throughout Rwanda between July 1993 and late 1994, this station broadcast extreme racial hatred toward the Tutsi ethnic minority. During the massacres of April–July 1994, RTLM broadcasts directly encouraged listeners to take part in the killing of Tutsi and moderate Hutu. In late 2003, two of the station's founders, John Bosco Barayagwiza and Ferdinand Nahimana were found guilty of genocide and other crimes against humanity by the International Criminal Tribunal for Rwanda in Arusha, Tanzania.

SEE ALSO: Movies; Music and musical instruments.

CLOTH PRODUCTION IS A TIME-HONORED TRADITION IN COASTAL EAST AFRICA. BUT, AS ELSEWHERE ON THE CONTINENT, THE TEXTILE INDUSTRY IN THE REGION IS NOW BEING BADLY HIT BY CHEAP IMPORTS.

HISTORY

Highland Ethiopia, the Red Sea coast, and the Indian Ocean coast have a long history of textile manufacture and trade. The Axumites in Ethiopia (c.100 B.C.E–700 C.E.) made their own cloth and also traded gold, ivory, slaves, and hides for fine cottons, linens, and silks. From the late seventh century, the coasts of Eritrea, Djibouti, and Somalia came under Arab influence and Arabian modes of dress were introduced. Arab influence reached the Swahili coast in the ninth century. Yet archaeological finds show that the Swahili also made their own cloth. Goods from the interior were exchanged by the Swahili for fine textiles, such as Chinese silks.

TEXTILES TODAY

Traditional rural dress is still widely worn in highland Ethiopia. It is made from cotton prepared and embroidered by women, but woven by men. Women's dress is usually in three parts: the *kamis* (a woven dress), *meknat* (a sash worn around the waist), and *netela* (a large cloak worn over the other two). The cotton is highly colorful and intricately embroidered. Weaving is also ceremonial, for example in making ornate wall hangings and tapestries for churches. Western styles have penetrated much of the region, though the coast remains influenced by Islam—notably in the plaid *ma'awis* (kilt), the *koofiyad* (embroidered cap) and *hijab* (head scarf).

On the Swahili coast brightly colored *kikois* and *kangas* are commonplace, worn either around the waist or wrapped around the head and shoulders. The *kanga* originated among Swahili women in the late 19th century. It comprises a large, square cotton cloth with a wide border (*pindo*), a central motif (*mji*), and a written Islamic proverb (*ujumbe*).

Today cheap imports from China and India are flooding the East African market. Kenya's small but thriving textile industry that focuses on export goods is finding it increasingly hard to compete globally.

*Brightly colored blankets (*shukka*) only became widespread among the Maasai in the 19th century. They were then the only form of clothing worn by this people and became their characteristic trademark. These Maasai women attending a ceremony are also adorned with beadwork jewelry.*

See also: Amhara; Maasai; Festival and ceremony; Swahili.

EAST AFRICAN BEADWORK

Beadwork is an ancient and highly prized tradition in East Africa. Different styles signify a person's ethnic group, social status, and stage of life. Nilotic girls wear elaborate beaded headdresses to display their readiness for marriage, while their mothers gain more beaded necklaces as they have more children. When Pokot mothers give birth, they are given an ornately beaded belt that is supposedly imbued with mystical powers that can aid their male children. Today, many bead workers include modern materials in their designs, such as metal wire and plastic beads. Tourist goods even include beadwork sandals, watchstraps, and cellphone covers.

TURKANA AND KARAMOJONG

FACT FILE

Population	Karamojong: 545,000, mostly in Uganda. Turkana: 500,000, mostly in Kenya
Religion	Preexisting beliefs, some Christianity
Language	Turkana and Karamojong are Atekar languages, which form part of the Eastern or Plains branch of Nilotic, closely related to Maasai and Samburu.

TIMELINE

c.1000	Early Eastern Nilotic speaking peoples move southward into northern Kenya.
c.1500	Turkana and Karamojong begin to expand into their present-day locations.
1850–1900	Turkana and Jie reorganize their age-set systems making them more militaristic.
1890–1900	First European explorers and colonialists arrive in the region.
1930s	Colonial attempts to secure the region.
1950s	First serious missionary attempts to convert the Turkana and Karamojong.
1960s	Serious droughts kill many Turkana herds. Ongoing ethnic conflict between armed groups in the region.
1971–79	Ugandan dictator Idi Amin orders massacre of 30,000 Karamojong for being a "primitive" people.
2000	Serious droughts spark further attempts to diversify the Turkana economy. International food relief efforts save many from starvation.
2001	Ugandan government begins program to disarm Karamojong of weapons kept as defense against cattle rustling.

K ARAMOJA, AN ARID PLATEAU ON THE KENYA–UGANDA BORDER, IS HOME TO THE RELATED AND FIERCELY INDEPENDENT TURKANA AND KARAMOJONG.

HISTORY

More than 1,000 years ago the ancestors of the modern Turkana and Karamojong began moving southward into the Lake Turkana region from their homeland in southern Sudan. Today the Turkana inhabit the vast plains around the southern shores of the lake in northern Kenya, while the Karamojong live in northwestern Uganda. The Karamojong actually comprise three distinct ethnic groupings, the Dodoso to the north, the Jie in the center, and the Karamojong to the south. The modern divisions, both between and within the Turkana and Karamojong, stem from the 19th century. Then a series of conflicts among these groups, their neighbors, and British colonial forces provoked major social upheaval. Successive colonial and national governments in Kenya and Uganda have tried to stamp their authority on these remote and highly mobile peoples.

Karamojong women build their own homes, weaving together straw and poles to make a framework, which they then cover with adobe (mud) bricks. The whole structure is then covered with a straw thatch.

A Turkana man (left) plays a pebble counting game known as ajua.

SOCIETY AND DAILY LIFE

The Turkana and Karamojong are renowned livestock herders who keep hardy, humped cattle known as zebu, goats, sheep, and some camels. They live chiefly from the blood and milk from their animals, although they also sometimes exchange their livestock for agricultural foodstuffs and fish. Blood is obtained by making a small cut in the neck of a cow with a special arrow. The blood is then collected in a gourd and the wound treated so that it quickly heals, causing relatively little discomfort to the animal. They are highly nomadic peoples, traveling great distances in search of water and grazing. They often build temporary villages, though the herds are generally kept on the move between temporary cattle camps.

Like most Nilotic peoples, the Turkana and Karamojong have never had chiefs. Rather, society is organized around lineages (extended families) and an age-grade system. Groups also bond by loaning each other livestock (see box feature). Following severe droughts in the 1960s, and more recently in 2000, there have been a number of official attempts to persuade the Turkana and Karamojong to take up a settled way of life and practice farming and fishing. However, these schemes have been spectacularly unsuccessful. This is because these peoples are firmly committed to a life of herding. Although they will diversify in times of crisis, when the crisis is over they will reinvest any profits in livestock, abandon settled farming, and go back to their pastoral lifestyle.

RELIGION AND CULTURE

Despite the best efforts of missionaries the Turkana and Karamojong have consistently resisted full conversion to Christianity. While many people are Christian in name, preexisting beliefs permeate most aspects of everyday life. The Karamojong and Turkana continue to believe in a single all-powerful god known as Akuj, who is commonly associated with the sun and is thought to reveal himself in natural occurrences such as thunder and lightning. Ancestral spirits are also important and sacrifices may be made both to them and to Akuj, particularly at special sites such as watering holed and sacred groves.

Like most Nilotic peoples, the Turkana and Karamojong remove boys' lower incisor teeth as an initiation rite. However, unlike the Kalenjin and Maasai, they do not practice circumcision. Rather, initiation among the Karamojong involves the rite of Asapan, in which a bull is slaughtered by the initiate and eaten communally.

STOCK LOANS AND SURVIVAL STRATEGIES

Mutual stock loans are a vitally important strategy among the Turkana and Karamojong. To help them overcome periods of drought, family cattle herds are often dispersed among relatives or special "stock friends." In this way, if one region is devastated, part of the herd will still survive. Stock loans are often also made to poor people or to young families trying to build up herds. People who enter into these arrangements are indebted, and may be asked to repay the favor at any time. Turkana and Karamojong society is thus characterized by intricate webs of personal relationships that unite people regardless of descent, age, and territory Such relationships are the key to survival on the arid Karamoja plains.

SEE ALSO: Nyoro; Oromo.

FACT FILE

Population	1.6 million in Malawi; 450,000 in Mozambique; 400,000 in Tanzania
Religion	Islam; Yao religion; some Christianity
Language	The Yao language, Chiyao, is an East Central Bantu tongue, and part of the wider Niger-Congo family.

TIMELINE

c.1650 Slave trade begins between the Yao and the East African coast Muslims.

1798 Earliest European accounts of the Yao, written in Portuguese by José de Laçerda.

c.1850 The Yao migrate into the regions they now occupy in Malawi and Tanzania.

1861 British Universities Mission to Central Africa established.

1866 Scottish Missionary David Livingstone visits the court of Yao chief Mataka.

1876 Church of Scotland Mission is established at Blantyre, just south of Lake Malawi.

1883 A British consul is established in the Yao region and the conflict over the slave trade intensifies.

1895 Kawinga, Matipwiri and Jalasi chiefs form an alliance against the British, but fail to prevent them suppressing the Yao slave trade.

1912 Many Yao are concentrated into larger settlements.

1964 Nyasaland gains independence from Britain, as Malawi.

1975 Mozambique, formerly Portuguese East Africa, achieves independence.

THE YAO COMPRISE SEVERAL PEOPLES LIVING AROUND LAKE MALAWI. THEY CURRENTLY INHABIT SOUTHEASTERN MALAWI, TANZANIA, AND NORTHERN MOZAMBIQUE.

HISTORY

The Yao traded with the Muslim peoples of the East African coast from the mid-17th century. Ivory and especially slaves were the main commodities. The Rovuma Valley, which lay in Yao territory, was the easiest route of communication between the coast and the African interior. The Portuguese encountered the Yao in the 18th century. In the 19th and 20th centuries Britain became the main colonial power in the area.

Missionaries such as David Livingstone, who visited the area in 1866, were the first British groups to settle in the region. Yet they immediately conflicted with the Yao over their involvement in the slave trade. Tensions escalated during the 1880s, and in 1895 an alliance between several Yao chiefdoms tried unsuccessfully to drive the British out of the region. By the following year the region was under firm British control.

Once colonial rule outlawed the slave trade, the Yao chiefs lost much of their authority and prestige. In the 20th century they were absorbed into the colonial administration of the area the British called Nyasaland. The chiefs were granted limited authority to govern and dispense justice, but were ultimately under central government control and had to collect taxes on behalf of the colonial authorities.

DAILY LIFE AND SOCIETY

The Yao are mainly a farming people whose most important food crops include corn, finger millet, sorghum, groundnuts, sweet potatoes, and rice. Cash crops, principally tobacco, are also grown for export. Other

important foodstuffs include fish (especially for those living along the shores of the lake) and insects. Before colonialism, hunting was also widespread, but has now largely died out. Few Yao keep cattle, since their territory is infested by the tsetse fly, bringing a high risk of livestock suffering from sleeping sickness (trypanosomasis). Yao men are generally responsible for building, cutting down trees, growing tobacco, and fishing. Women carry out domestic duties such as cooking, sweeping, beer-making, potting, and hoeing the ground in preparation for planting.

Although the Yao have chiefs, they have never been a unified political power or ever formed a larger centralized kingdom. They are generally a matrilineal people, meaning that they trace their family descent through the female line. Positions of political power are therefore inherited by a man from his mother's brother, rather than his father. Strong ties exist between Yao brothers and sisters and after marriage, a man—unless he is a headman or a chief—usually goes to live with his wife's family rather than vice versa.

CULTURE AND RELIGION

Through their past contacts with Muslim merchants along the East African coast the Yao have been heavily influenced by Islam. Widespread conversion took place in the 19th century. As a result, many Yao have resisted Christian attempts to convert them. The main Muslim rituals, such as daily prayer and fasting during the holy month of Ramadan are observed. However, in some areas preexisting religious practices remain important and have been mixed with Islam.

The veneration of ancestors (*makosa*) is central to Yao religion. Communication between the living and the dead was the responsibility of the chiefs. Witchcraft is a constant source of fear for many Yao, and diviners are regularly employed to identify sorcerers, who are believed to eat human flesh. Unlike many other African peoples, the Yao do not believe in a supreme Creator God.

SEE ALSO: Christianity; Islam; Swahili.

Yao people on the southern shores on Lake Malawi. The plentiful fish fished from the lake form an important part of the Yao diet.

LUPANDA INITIATION

Initiation ceremonies for Yao boys, which are known as *lupanda*, are performed once a year. They are carried out under the supervision of a figure of authority such as a chief. Initiates, mostly between 7 and 11 years old, gather at a designated site, where the chief ritually dusts them with flour carried in a special basket called a *ciselo*. Dancing and masquerades accompany the ceremony. The next day the boys are taken away from the *lupanda* area and circumcized. Over several months they are taught the skills and knowledge they will need as grown men. After completing his initiation a Yao man is given a new name and it is considered a major insult to call him by the name he had as a child.

Any of the words printed in SMALL CAPITAL LETTERS can be looked up in this glossary.

adobe Dried clay or mud, widely used as a building material throughout Africa.

age-grades The different social level in certain societies. Each person is part of an "age-set" (a group of similar-aged peers) who move up as they grow older through the various age-grades, gaining in status.

agriculturalist A settled (sedentary) farmer who makes his or her living by cultivating crops.

asaimara Historically, the politically dominant group among the Afar people. The subordinate class is called the "adoimara."

askari African troops who were conscripted into the colonial armies of German East Africa during World War I (1914–18).

bridewealth A common practice among African peoples, in which a marriage is sealed by a gift given by the groom to the family of the bride. This gift is often in the form of cattle, but may also be other livestock or money.

bugalli A stiff porridge or flatbread made from corn flour. It is a widespread staple food in East Africa.

clan A social group made up of several extended families or LINEAGES. Clan members often trace their descent from a common ancestor.

Derg Popular term for the hardline Marxist regime of Mengistu Haile Mariam, in power in Ethiopia from 1974 to 1991.

dhow A cargo-carrying sailboat with a raised deck at the stern, long used for transporting goods in the Gulf of Arabia, Red Sea, the east coast of Africa, and the Indian Ocean.

Eunoto A RITE OF PASSAGE ceremony among the Maasai of Kenya and Tanzania, marking the initiation of young men into adulthood. It is accompanied by dancing and singing.

gebbar A feudal system of land tenure and taxation practiced by the Amhara of Ethiopia until 1974. It involved peasants growing what crops they wished but donating a percentage of their produce to a local landowner.

Ge'ez An ancient Semitic language related to Amharic; it is now only used in religious services of the Ethiopian Orthodox Christian Church.

hadith A narrative record of the sayings and customs of Muhammad and his companions, forming a body of Muslim traditions.

hajj The annual pilgrimage to the holy city of Mecca in Saudi Arabia to pray at Islam's holiest shrine, the Kaaba, and undertake other religious duties. It is one of the Five Pillars (essential holy duties) of Islam, and so long as a person has the means to do so, she or he is expected to undertake the journey at least once during his or her lifetime.

hominid A member of the mammalian family Hominidae, relatively large-brained primates that walked upright on their hind legs (that is, were bipedal). Some species of hominids, known as australopithecines, are considered ancestral to humans. Their fossils have been discovered at sites in East and southern Africa, plus one find in Chad.

indentured laborer A person drafted on a fixed, low-wage contract to work abroad on a specified task or major project. Many Indians, for example, were brought to East Africa by the British colonial authorities to build railroads.

infibulation The custom of female circumcision (also called female genital mutilation). It is practiced by some African peoples, and involves sewing up the vulva. It is harmful to a girl's health and is strongly discouraged by health authorities and aid workers. Some countries have outlawed the practice.

Interahamwe The Hutu militias, trained by the Rwandan military in 1993–94 to commit genocide against the country's Tutsi population, killing 800,000 people in three months. Many fled to neighboring countries to escape justice.

jihad (Arabic: "struggle") In Islam, the struggle a person undertakes to submit to Allah. It may involve armed struggle, and so is often translated as "holy war." Some Muslim authorities see it as a sixth "pillar," or basic duty of Islam.

kabaka The ruler of the kingdom of Baganda.

kanga A brightly colored and patterned two-piece cotton garment traditionally worn by Swahili women. Swahili proverbs may often be incorporated within the design.

kessim The religious authorities and community leaders of the Jewish people of Ethiopia, the Beta Israel, or Falasha.

kikoi A cloth worn wrapped around the waist by Swahili men.

kok A council of clan elders among the Kalenjin people of Kenya.

laibon A prophet, healer, and diviner of the Maasai people.

lineage An extended family group that shares a common ancestor. If the society traces its origins to a male ancestor and descent is traced from father to son, the lineage is termed patrilineal. If the ancestor is female and descent traced from mother to daughter, the lineage is matrilineal.

lost-wax casting A metal-casting technique used in Africa. It involves making a wax model of the object to be cast and encasing it in a clay mold. When the mold is heated, the wax melts and molten metal is then poured into the cavity through a hole in the mold.

masjid The name for a synagogue among the Beta Israel (Falasha), the Jewish people of Ethiopia.

Mau Mau A secret society founded in 1948–49 among the Kikuyu, Meru, and Embu peoples of Kenya to fight against British colonial rule. It began a campaign of intimidation in 1952. Brutal repression by the British authorities, including mass detentions, brought the uprising under control by 1956.

mondo mogo A medicine man of the Kikuyu, who is responsible for finding out the cause of illness.

moran An AGE-GRADE among the Maasai, denoting young men who have undergone initiation and circumcision and are put in charge of herding livestock. Formerly, they were also warriors.

mosque An Islamic place of worship.

mugongo In the Bunyoro region of Uganda, home of the Nyoro people, a ridge of raised ground surrounded by swampy streams. These places were the sites of Nyoro settlement, with a single CLAN occupying each ridge.

nomad (adj: nomadic) A person who follows a wandering lifestyle, usually living either by herding livestock or trading. The movements of nomads, such as the Bedouin or Tuareg of the Sahara, are determined by the need to find new grazing pastures, or by trade demands.

nyatiti An eight-stringed traditional lyre, used by Kenyan musicians.

omukama The ruler of the kingdom of Bunyoro.

pastoralist A person who lives by herding livestock such as cattle or sheep, often as part of a nomadic or seminomadic life.

polygyny The practice of marrying more than one wife.

Quran The holy book of the Islamic faith. It consists of verses (*surahs*) and is regarded by Muslims as a direct transcription of the Word of God (Allah) recited to Muhammad by the angel Jibril (Gabriel).

Ramadan The ninth month of the Islamic calendar, held holy by Muslims as the month during which Allah called Muhammad to be His Prophet. Muslims fast between sunrise and sunset during Ramadan. The end of the month is marked by a major celebration known as Eid ul-Fitr.

reliquary (adj. and noun) A container used to hold the remains of a person, or a term to describe such a vessel.

riika An AGE-GRADE among the Kikuyu of Kenya.

rite of passage A ceremony, such as initiation into adulthood or marriage, that marks the passage of a person from one stage of life to another.

ruoth A clan chief of the Luo people.

savanna Tropical grassland dominated by various species of perennial grasses interspersed with varying numbers of shrubs and low trees. Much of tropical East Africa is characterized by this terrain.

shantytown An area of impermanent housing, usually made from scrap materials, on the outskirts of large cities where poor migrants to urban areas live. Shantytowns often lack running water, drainage, and other basic amenities.

Sharia (Arabic: "divine law") Islamic law. Sharia is based both on the edicts established by the Prophet Muhammad in the QURAN and on the practices that Muhammad observed during his lifetime, which later Islamic scholars formulated as guidelines regulating the lives of Muslims.

shifting cultivation A farming method (once termed "slash-and-burn" agriculture) that involves clearing an area of forest for temporary crop growing. After harvesting the crop, the farmers move on to a new location.

stele (plural: "stelae") A carved obelisk. In Ethiopia, the huge stelae at Axum in highland Ethiopia are the remains of a civilization that flourished there around 100–700 C.E.

subsistence farming A type of agriculture in which all the crops grown are eaten by the farmer and his family, leaving nothing to sell for profit ("cash crops") at market.

Sufism A branch of Islam whose followers, known as Sufis or dervishes, follow a path of strict self-discipline and devote themselves to prayer in an attempt to know Allah directly through mystical experience. Some dervish sects are known for their trancelike whirling dances.

Taarab (or Tarabu) A form of Swahili poetry set to music. Originally an Islamic form, it has been greatly adapted.

taboo A restriction or prohibition in a culture, established by convention, which prevents a person from acting in ways seen as inappropriate. Many taboos relate to tasks that must not be undertaken by one sex or the other, food that must not be eaten, or certain forms of clothing that may not be worn.

tabot A replica of the Biblical Ark of the Covenant (the receptacle used to hold the Ten Commandments that God gave to Moses), used in all Orthodox churches in Ethiopia and paraded at the festival of TIMKAT.

Talmud (Hebrew: "learning") A collection of interpretations of Jewish civil and religious law, based on oral teachings.

tariqa A Muslim brotherhood; in Somalia, they are often associated with SUFISM and act as centers of Islamic teaching. In the early 20th century, these institutions were active in opposing colonialism.

teff A small cultivated cereal grain widely grown in Ethiopia.

Tewahido The Orthodox Christian Church in Ethiopia.

Timkat The name for Epiphany—the festival on January 6 commemorating the revelation of Jesus as the Risen Lord—in the Orthodox Christian Church in Ethiopia.

Torah The first five books of the Old Testament, comprising the Hebrew Bible. The term also refers to the whole body of traditional Jewish teaching.

tsetse fly An insect that carries parasites that pass disease to both people and cattle. It is widespread in East and Central Africa, and is responsible for the spread of sleeping sickness (trypanosomasis).

ujamaa (Swahili: "togetherness") A state cooperative farming village established in Tanzania as a result of the VILLAGIZATION program announced in the Arusha Declaration of 1967. The term is also used for a form of Makonde sculpture.

urbanization The process by which a rural area becomes more built-up and industrialized. This generally involves the migration of rural people into cities.

villagization The process of restructuring rural communities into planned villages, often run by a cooperative and controlled by the state. President Julius Nyerere introduced villagization to Tanzania in the late 1960s and early 1970s.

wattle-and-daub A building technique that uses clay plastered on a latticework made of sticks.

waungwana In traditional Swahili society, the noble merchant families that controlled Indian Ocean trade. These families were powerful and wealthey and observed a strict hierarchy.

zebu A hardy form of cattle with a characteristic humped back, widely kept by peoples in sub-Saharan Africa. It can exist on relatively poor grazing land.

General books:

Beckwith, C., and Fisher, A. *African Ceremonies* (Harry N. Abrams, Inc., New York, NY, 2002).

Hynson, C. *Exploration of Africa* (Barrons Juveniles, Hauppauge, NY, 1998).

Mitchell, P. J. *African Connections: Archaeological Perspectives on Africa and the Wider World* (AltaMira Press, Walnut Creek, CA, 2005).

Morris, P., Barrett, A., Murray, A., and Smits van Oyen, M. *Wild Africa* (BBC, London, UK, 2001).

Murray, J. *Africa: Cultural Atlas for Young People* (Facts On File, New York, NY, 2003).

Philips, T. (ed.) *Africa: The Art of a Continent* (Prestel, Munich, Germany, 1995).

Rasmussen, R. K. *Modern African Political Leaders* (Facts On File, New York, NY, 1998).

Reader, J. *Africa: A Biography of the Continent* (Penguin, New York, NY, 1998).

Sheehan, S. *Great African Kingdoms* (Raintree/Steck-Vaughn, Austin, TX, 1998).

Stuart, C., and Stuart, T. *Africa—A Natural History* (Swan Hill Press, Shrewsbury, UK, 1995).

Temko, F. *Traditional Crafts from Africa* (Lerner Publishing, Minneapolis, MN, 1996).

The Diagram Group *Encyclopedia of African Peoples* (Facts On File, New York, NY, 2000).

The Diagram Group *Encyclopedia of African Nations and Civilizations* (Facts On File, New York, NY, 2003).

Thomas, V. M. *Lest We Forget: The Passage from Africa to Slavery and Emancipation* (Crown Publishers, New York, NY, 1997).

Books specific to this volume:

Berg, E. *Ethiopia (Countries of the World)* (Gareth Stevens Publishing, Milwaukee, WI, 2000).

Giles, B. *Kenya* (Raintree/Steck-Vaughn, Austin, TX, 2001).

Goodall, J. *In the Shadow of Man* (Houghton Miffin Co., Boston, MA, 1988).

Hetfield, J. *The Maasai of East Africa* (Rosen Publishing Group, New York, NY, 2003).

Horton, M., and Middleton, J. *The Swahili* (Blackwells, Oxford, UK, 2001).

Smith, A., *The Great Rift—Africa's Changing Valley* (BBC, London, 1988).

The Diagram Group *History of East Africa* (Facts On File, New York, NY, 2003).

Wilson, T. H. *City States of the Swahili Coast* (Franklin Watts, Danbury, CT, 1998).

Useful Web sites:

www.africa.upenn.edu/NEH/tethnic.htm
University of Pennsylvania African Studies Group online encyclopedia of East Africa.

www.cyberethiopia.com
Resources on Ethiopia.

www.eac.int
Official Web site of the East African Community.

gbmna.org/index.php
The Green Belt Movement, a nongovernmental organization founded by Nobel laureate Wangari Maathai.

www.janegoodall.org
Jane Goodall Institute for conservation, springing from her pioneering work in Tanzania with chimpanzees.

www.kenyaweb.com
Resources on Kenya.

www.maasaierc.org
Maasai environmental and human rights campaign group.

www.tzonline.org
Resources on Tanzania.

www.yale.edu/gsp/rwanda
One of many sites with information on the Rwandan genocide.

PICTURE CREDITS